Growing the Soul

MEDITATIONS FROM MY GARDEN

Delia Halverson

*Then each of you will live at peace
and entertain your friends in your own vineyard
and under your own fig trees.
—Zachariah 3:10 (CEV)*

DIMENSIONS
FOR LIVING
NASHVILLE

GROWING THE SOUL: MEDITATIONS FROM MY GARDEN

Library of Congress Cataloging-in-Publication Data

Halverson, Delia Touchton.
  Growing the soul : meditations from my garden / Delia Halverson.
    p. cm.
  ISBN 0-687-06267-5
  1. Gardeners—Prayer-books and devotions—English. 2. Gardens—
  Religious aspects—Christianity—Meditations. 3. Devotional calendars.
  I. Title.

  BV4596.G36H35 2005
  242'.68—dc22

2004025516

05 06 07 08 09 10 11 12 13 14—10 9 8 7 6 5 4 3 2 1

MANUFACTURED IN THE UNITED STATES OF AMERICA

To all my gardening friends

—past, present, and future

Contents

MY GARDEN HOLDS HIDDEN JOYS

MY GARDEN PROVIDES LESSONS FOR LIFE

MY GARDEN GIVES SABBATH TIME

MY GARDEN SMOOTHS OUT ROUGH EDGES

MY GARDEN RECYCLES LIFE

MY GARDEN OPPORTUNITIES, LOST AND FOUND

Introduction

My first year away from home and dorm life, my husband and I lived in a basement apartment with no garden. But I enjoyed houseplants, and each weekend we traveled to my mother-in-law's home where I could dig in the dirt to my heart's content. In all fourteen homes since then, we have always had a garden of some type. With our most recent move we considered a condo, but I could not imagine life without my garden. When we visit our Ohio grandchildren, we help them in their garden, and now as I care for our infant granddaughters each day, I am preparing them for life in a garden.

Jesus enjoyed gardens. He often taught in the outdoors, surrounded by nature. The Gospel writers often referred to times when Jesus went away to be alone. When he was struggling with the most difficult decision of his life, he sought out the beauty and solitude of the Garden of Gethsemane, which was probably a garden he had enjoyed on other trips to Jerusalem.

Gardens have been a part of life from the beginning of time. The whole world is our garden, but in our industrialization we have destroyed much of it with "signs of progress." Gardens are even more important now. They give us rest from the "progress" that tends to leave us speechless. They are spots of renewal. They are reminders of relationships. They hold hidden joys and smooth out rough edges in our lives.

As I work in my garden, I often paraphrase a hymn, singing: "My God and I work in my garden together. . . . " The garden is truly one of the best places I find to be close to God. I hope that this little book helps you come to similar experiences with God.

Delia Halverson

My Garden Creates Friendships

– 1 –

Welcome to My Garden

Be sure to welcome strangers into your home. By doing this, some people have welcomed angels as guests, without even knowing it.

—Hebrews 13:2

I would hesitate to guess just how many different types of gardens there are. It seems that every country has its own style of garden. Some gardens are in the midst of open fields and some are in courtyards hidden behind walls. Some gardens are formal affairs, with each plant carefully manicured and growing in its special place, and some are a hodgepodge of plants reflecting the gardener's whim at the time. Some contain only specific types of plants, such as rose gardens and herb gardens, and some are as varied as an artist's palette. There are desert gardens and water gardens, vegetable gardens and bonsai gardens. There are butterfly gardens, and even gardens planted specifically for deer.

In addition, each person who develops a garden makes it uniquely his or hers. There is an unusual garden that I pass by regularly. Each time I go by I see something in the garden that I hadn't seen before. It contains everything from a department store mannequin to an old dish antenna; from a rusted basketball hoop to a rocking chair with the seat missing. Shovels without handles parade along the border of one planting bed, and a child's plastic swimming pool is filled with numerous plants. You feel as if you know the owner by observing all of the strategically placed decorations.

Our family lived in the Dakotas for thirteen years. One of my favorite pictures that I discovered while living there was titled "The Prairie Is My Garden." In the picture a pioneer woman and child are gathering wildflowers in front of their simple home.

No matter what the style, I believe a garden must be made hospitable and welcoming in order for its plants to thrive. I cannot command and force a plant to grow. It is not my green thumb that makes this happen. But I can pull the weeds around the plant. I can provide water and fertilizer. I can make sure that plants have the appropriate sunlight. This hospitality to a plant allows it to reach out and stretch its roots.

Likewise, I cannot command the soul of a person to grow, but I can help create an atmosphere in which it can. Creating a hospitable garden also means preparing the surroundings so that others feel comfortable and can reach out to God and grow their souls. It is inviting; it says, "Come and rest awhile. Leave your cares behind and spend some time away." The garden may have secluded places where a person can seek solitude, but even those places say, "Welcome."

Whether your garden is several acres in size or simply a deck or patio with container plantings, it is important to make it hospitable. View it from another's perspective. Does it invite people into the space? Does it say, "You can find God here"?

Reflect

~ What gardens have you seen that were forbidden?

~ What gardens have you entered where you felt the presence of God?

~ How can you make your garden more hospitable and a ministry to share with others?

Pray

I thank you, God, for creating a welcoming world. Help me be hospitable to others by welcoming them into the gardens of my soul. Amen.

– 2 –

Gardening Neighbors

We should try to live at peace and help each other have a strong faith.
—Romans 14:19

Agardening friend is as precious as gold. But to discover a neighbor who has never gardened and who becomes a gardening friend is like discovering a rock that turns out to be a diamond! Such was the case in one community where we lived.

We purchased a house with nothing on the lot except the two small trees in front of the house that came with the landscape package. On one side was a tall fence, erected to contain a friendly dog named Lucky.

In the fifteen moves I've made in my adult life, I've always managed to take some plants from one garden to another, and this time was no exception. This move had involved a six-month period of "homelessness" while our house was built, but I'd found a temporary home for pots of plants in a friend's yard. Now they had a true home, and I began placing them at strategic spots around the yard.

Soon I discovered my neighbor experimenting with her first garden, and I shared some plants with her. She purchased more plants and shared with me. As the plants grew, our friendship across the fence grew. Along with our daylilies and milkweed seedlings, we were able to share our joys and sorrows. Sometimes it was only a word or two across the fence, and sometimes it involved longer conversations as we moved seedlings from one yard to the other. Through the years, as seedling trees became twenty-foot giants (this was Florida!) and butterflies flittered across the fence, our uncommon friendship became strong and true.

I firmly believe that God created us to be in community with one another. If that were not the case, we would be self-sustaining, like some animals. Although you occasionally run across a Robinson Crusoe, most of us find that we do better when we surround ourselves with friends we can depend on, friends to help us face life, and friends with whom we can grow.

I've found that gardening brings such friends together, as long as the gardens are based on friendships and not on competition.

Reflect

~ What gardening friends have you had? What, besides plants, have you shared?

~ Whom do you know who needs a friend, perhaps not a gardening friend, but a friend who would enjoy your garden?

~ How can you use your garden to develop friendships?

Pray

Thank you, God, for creating us with a need for friends. Show me ways to live at peace with others and to help them with their faith. Amen.

– 3 –

Garden Magic

Our LORD, by your wisdom you made so many things; the whole earth is covered with your living creatures.

—Psalm 104:24

Gardens are such special places, whether you are working in them or simply enjoying them. Their power can create friendships, and through those friendships "magic" can happen.

There is a classic book titled *The Secret Garden* (by Frances Hodgson Burnett) that tells what can happen in a garden. In the book a young troubled orphan, Mary, meets a boy, Dickon, in the secret garden. Dickon knows the power of caring and shares it with Mary. This power changes her, and she in turn shares the power with a boy, Colin, who is sick not only physically but also emotionally. The garden's caring power transforms Colin, and when the day comes that he can stand up from his wheelchair, Dickon teaches him to sing praises to God with the doxology. In the book, the word *magic* is used as a metaphor for the mystery and awe we feel about God, the Creator. In reality, magic is built on illusion. But in this use of the term, magic is that attitude of awe about that power which we do not know but which we call God. How we feel about magic, in this sense, is much like the way we feel about worship.

Garden Magic

We sometimes feel that we must know all that there is to know about God. We delve into books of theology and search out the wise sages of our day, looking for all the answers. We want every aspect of nature explained. By doing this we often miss the real mystery of God. We miss the "magic" because we are busy explaining. We miss the opportunity to simply stand in the garden, in the presence of God, and sing:

> Praise God, from whom all blessings flow;
> Praise God, all creatures here below;
> Praise God above, ye heavenly host;
> Creator, Son, and Holy Ghost. Amen.

Reflect

~ How can anyone explain the power that pushes a root into the ground or the power that causes something as tender as a leaf to burst open the shell of a seed? How is experiencing such a power a way to worship God?

~ How is that power a part of your life?

~ What magic do you find in a garden?

~ How can you share that magic, and with it share God with someone else?

Pray

God of the garden, reveal your magic in the garden and give me appreciation for the awe that surrounds me there. Help me find ways to pass that experience of worship on to someone else through your gardens. Amen.

– 4 –

Friendship and Hope

Jesus looked straight at them and said, "There are some things that people cannot do, but God can do anything."

—Matthew 19:26

I was delighted when a group I belong to announced that at the next meeting we were to bring a plant to exchange. I had not had many opportunities to exchange plants since my last move. I potted several starts of herbs and perennials. At the last minute, I grabbed some small "hen and chicks." I had received a small start of this plant from my son, who got his start from his mother-in-law. This plant produces smaller versions of itself all around the motherplant. I took several of the small shoots that had grown around the larger plant. The hen and chicks were a hit, and friendships were deepened.

The gift I received in the exchange was a lovely purple lantana, spilling over the edges of the pot. Although purple is a bright color in any garden, I decided to leave this lantana in its pot and place it on the deck. One evening, several weeks later, I noticed that the plant was completely wilted. The leaves even seemed brittle. I checked the condition of the soil, and evidently I had missed it the last time I watered. I held little hope for the plant's survival. I had put it through some real trauma. If it did survive, I was certain it would have to put out completely new growth. But I filled the watering can and drenched its roots anyway.

With the morning came hope! The plant had lifted its purple flower heads, and the leaves had become lush and limber. What more could I ask? What appeared to be dead was now alive.

I remembered that Jesus had told a story of hope about a father and his two sons. We usually think of it as a story of forgiveness, and that it is. But the story of two sons in Luke 15:11-24 is also one of hope—hope lost and hope returned. It tells of the hope of a father for his two sons and how one son left. When a son leaves in such circumstances, the parent is likely to lose hope, but not this father. He continued to hope for the son's return. According to Jewish tradition, such a disobedient son should have been disowned, but despite the tradition his father continued to hope, watching for the return of his son.

The story also speaks of the hope of the son when he had spent all he had been given and was living a desolate life. When he came to his senses, his only hope was that his father would take him in as a servant. He was prepared to ask for such a concession. Can you imagine the surprise when his father rushed to welcome him and dressed him as royalty? Here the hope of forgiving love was kindled. Here was death come to life. As the father said, "This son of mine was dead, but has now come back to life."

My lantana evidently is a very forgiving plant. There are such plants, just as there are such fathers. Although the boy knew that he had wronged his father, he also know the type of man his father was, and he knew that he could ask for forgiveness. The father allowed God's love to work through him, to forgive and continue to love his son. If we know that forgiveness is possible, then we can have hope. God's grace and forgiveness give us new life, like the new chance of the son in the story. God was at work too. In God we have our hope, and in God hope comes about.

Reflect

~ When have you almost given up hope and then had hope to shine through?

~ How can you help others maintain hope in times of trouble?

~ Whom can you forgive and help restore hope to?

Pray

God of hope, we sometimes flounder in our desperation. There are times when all hope seems lost. Give us the courage to know that all things are possible with you. Although things may not turn out the way we had dreamed, we know that you are our true source of hope and fulfillment. Amen.

– 5 –

Sharpening Brings Clarity

Just as iron sharpens iron, friends sharpen the minds of each other.
—Proverbs 27:17

After years of digging, my favorite shovel balked each time I put it into the ground. This little digging implement was just the right height for me, measuring about four feet long with a handle at the top. It was not a tool for moving mammoth amounts of dirt, but then I've never moved that much dirt. Just as I was prepared to give up on the shovel, my husband brought out a file and sharpened it. Metal on metal made a difference. Now the shovel was as good as new!

The wisdom in this verse from Proverbs is as true for friends as it is for iron. Sometimes we think that friends should always agree on everything. In fact, often we seek out friends who have minds attuned to ours. But this does not always promote growth. If we limit our friendships to persons who agree with us, then we become stagnant. Friendly clashes of opinion can help us explore new ideas and sharpen our minds.

The trouble comes when we forget that no one has a monopoly on understanding. If any of us knew all the answers, then we would be God. What is right for me may not be right for you, and I must respect your right to your own opinion. Each of us is formed by our experiences and by those whom we encounter, and my experiences and relationships have been different from yours. Likewise, what was right for me five years ago may not be right for me today.

Growth comes when we are open to listening to all sides of an issue, rather than simply looking for a soapbox on which to stand and spout our own opinions. True dialogue involves give and take on all sides and allows for differences to exist without cutting off communication and relationship.

Each time I turn over a shovel full of dirt with my sharpened shovel, I remember the scraping noise that comes from metal on metal. Each time I turn a new idea over in my head, I appreciate the friend who brought it to my attention.

Reflect

~ Whom do you know who allows you to sharpen your mind with his or hers?

~ How can you approach a discussion with the understanding that you will probably disagree, but still remain friends?

~ What book have you read recently that might make a good discussion starter with a friend, even though you may disagree?

Pray

Help me, Lord, to approach those who disagree with me openly. Give me the wisdom to invite them to agree or disagree at times. Sharpen my mind by putting such opportunities before me. Amen.

– 6 –

Moving On

The LORD said to Abram: Leave your country, your family, and your relatives and go to the land that I will show you.

—Genesis 12:1

When our daughter was a toddler she had the nicest red and black rubber boots. They slipped on without shoes and kept her feet dry and clean. We lived in a small South Dakota town (population less than 100) that turned to mud when it rained or when the snow melted. One spring she followed her brother and his friend into the remains of the previous year's garden. I'm not sure what they were looking for, but it was a time of adventure. When I heard the cries of distress, I rushed to the garden to find her stuck in the mud, almost to the boot tops. There was no way she was going to get out of the garden muck alone. I had to lift her, literally, out of her boots and place her on firm ground. We had to leave the boots in the mud.

Like Abraham, I've had to leave places I've lived, and sometimes my family and relatives, and go to another land. Sometimes it has been my choice and sometimes someone else's, but it's always been with a sense that the move was a part of God's desire for me at that time. I've also left behind, in the mud, some parts of my life. The parts of my life left in the mud might have been a friendship or a job, or a relationship that never got resolved. It might have been a house we've built or remodeled, or a church family we'd grown to love. And there has always been a garden I've left behind, because I create gardens everywhere I go. I kept in contact with friends. I worked to resolve a relationship. But I had to realize that we must move onward. Sometimes we must leave things behind, accepting them and moving onward. We must use the "mud" of the past to grow the blooms of the future.

Mud is not always a bad thing! In fact, good things can come from what appears to be bad. The garden mud contains all the nutrients needed to grow our vegetables and bring blooms to the flowers. I've often said that my parents brainwashed me into believing that moving was an adventure. What would our next house be like? What hidden treasures would we find in the garden that someone else planted? What sort of neighbors would we discover? Who would be our new friends in school? And what did God have in store for us at the new place? I learned not to dwell on the past. I learned to look forward, to expect and anticipate what God was prepared to do in my new life. I had new boots to wear and new gardens to tend. There would be new roads to roam and new friends to make.

Although the muck of my past gardens holds many fond memories, I've found that each new garden has its own nutritious dirt, ready to be cultivated. The blooms of friendship and the fruits of ministry will grow in the new place as well as in the old. They may have a slightly different color or taste, but God gives them the growth, with my help along the way.

Reflect

~ What are some of the things lodged in the muck of the past that you need to leave behind?

~ How can you release those things and put on new boots?

~ What new land, new responsibility, new friendship is God calling you to today?

Pray

Give me the peace, O God, to recognize what I must let go of in my life. Help me respond to your call and, like Abram, move forward with confidence. Amen.

– 7 –

The Common Branch

I am the vine, and you are the branches. If you stay joined to me, and I stay joined to you, then you will produce lots of fruit. But you cannot do anything without me.

—John 15:5

Aburst of red blooms covers the rosebush climbing the trellis at the corner of my house. This rosebush was the first gift for our new home from our daughter. Now, a year and a half later, it is a solid bank of crimson roses. The blooms are so close together that it looks like one massive splash of color from a paintbrush.

These blooms remind me of the many friends we have accumulated in our moves, from high school classmates to a friend in her mid eighties who continues to teach youth Sunday school. Just as our climbing rose makes new branches every year, our Christmas letter list continues to grow. Although we barely kept in contact with some of our friends during the intervening years, the memories of our friendship were so important that it was worth the stamp each year to stay in touch. Then, suddenly, one of us remembers an incident or a word that we shared, and the friendship is rekindled.

Each time I hold a cup of coffee between my palms on a cold day I remember North Dakota mornings and Cathy, who said, "The only reason I drink coffee is to warm my hands." When I see a splash of yellow daffodils each spring, I remember Bobbie in Idaho, who cut them from her yard and sent a bouquet with her physician husband when he came to attend me at the birth of my daughter. When I knit a baby blanket, I remember Una and Phyllis in Minnesota, who learned to knit with me. When I see a Christmas tree farm, I remember Bob in South Dakota, who laughed at the antics of our family when he went with us to cut a Christmas tree in the forest. When I sit on the deck on a spring morning, I remember Sue in Georgia, to whom we called our greetings across the banisters of neighboring decks. When I share a plant, I remember Joy in Florida, who was my gardening neighbor. And on and on it goes—the memories and the friends.

All these friends are branches of my life memory. But even more than that, I recognize that all these friends are connected to me through Christ. That is a constant in our relationship. Without that root, we cannot be productive.

Christ has promised that we will bear fruit, that we will bring forth a blaze of crimson in the world, if we remain connected to him. I've found it true. When I cut a branch off my rose and bring it into the house, I place it in water. It looks alive for a period of time, but eventually it begins to wither. First the petals fade, and then even the leaves dry up and fall off. All that is left is a stiff branch with prickly thorns. By then it is useless, and I cast it out. But if I had left that same branch on the vine, it would have produced flowers year after year. The amazing thing that does not hold true in this metaphor is that, with Christ, we can be rejoined to the vine. We can be rejoined to Christ because of God's grace-type love, a love that says "I may not like something that you do, but I'll always love you no matter what." That love has no parallel in a metaphor of a climbing rose.

Life is constant and much fuller when we stay connected to the vine. The roots go deep, and even in drought there is nourishment.

Reflect

~ Who are the blooms of friendship in your past? How are you commonly connected with Christ?

~ When have you felt that you were cut off from your soul's life source and then found that you could be rejoined?

~ What can you do to make sure that you keep the connection to Christ?

Pray

I thank you, God, for the persons who have kept me constant—faithful, connected, and steady—with you. Help me enable others to live in relationship with you and with all that you created. Amen.

My Garden Is a Sacred Space

– 8 –

Garden Night Lights

I often think of the heavens your hands have made, and of the moon and stars you put in place.

—Psalm 8:3

It was a once-in-a-lifetime experience, we were told. They advertised the event energetically on television. We were to look up into the sky and observe a blaze of stars shooting across the heavens. But despite their daily reminders, I was dressed for bed before I remembered the event. Yet I hated to miss the experience of a lifetime, and so I grabbed a large beach towel and headed out the door and into my garden in my pajamas.

Although I was only a house away from a very busy road, my garden was rather secluded from view so I decided it worth the risk. Making sure all the lights on the back side of the house were turned off, I spread my beach towel on the grass and lay on my back to observe the demonstration.

True to the advertisement, God did put on a brilliant display. Across the sky streaked first one star and then another, sometimes leaving a trail of luminescence—at least in my mind's eye. How could a light, racing across the heavens many miles above, seem so close? And to make it even more infinite, the stardust our earth was moving through had been left as debris from a comet. I'm told that when a bit of this debris enters the atmosphere it is traveling at 30,000 miles per hour, compressing air in front of it so that it heats up to 3000° Fahrenheit. I can barely fathom this; it is beyond my limited understanding!

I am certainly no scientist. In fact, science was one of my worst subjects in school. But I know the display I saw was like incandescent rain, twisting and turning through high-altitude winds. Only a great God could create the matter that caused the display that night. And to think, that God is also my partner in creation as I dig in the dirt of my garden!

Reflect

~ Recall times when you have experienced a powerful display of God's creation.

~ When have you felt awed by small parts of God's creation?

~ How do you feel, realizing that the God who created such magnificence also created you and seeks to have a personal relationship with you?

Pray

God of the sky, come and stand over my shoulder as I dig in the dirt. Amen.

– 9 –

Ever-flowing Garden Streams

Let justice roll down like waters, and righteousness like an everflowing stream.

—Amos 5:24 NRSV

It was a garden in the foothills of the mountains. I had dug and raked the red Georgia clay, fighting to make an old roadbed palatable for my bulbs and seeds. I had combed the woods nearby for native ferns and violets to accent the foreign plants I had brought in. It had been a long time coming, but now the garden was growing well.

From where I stood in the garden, I could see the lake nestled between the hills with the sun glistening off the surface. Our resident geese swam in the cove nearby, and a chorus of frogs sang in a swampy area. A very pleasant scene indeed, and my physical labor was making it even more pleasant.

As lovely as the lake and garden were, the most unique thing about this plot was the constant ripple of a rocky creek just beyond the garden's boundary. It reminded me that gardens are for all the senses. This one pleased not only the eyes, but also the ears.

As I pulled a muddy water hose from one bed to another, I began to reflect on water. During a dry spell, my garden depended on me to deliver the water. I had introduced plants that were not locally adapted to this particular environment, so when the dry spells came the plants would dry up and die if I did not water them. Yet, less than a hundred feet away was a constant stream of water, joyfully making its way to the lake.

I knew there were people in other parts of the world who carry their drinking water for miles each day, sometimes walking two hours or more each way. And I complained about dragging hoses to keep my garden alive!

As I listened to the stream, I thought about the scripture in Amos about "justice roll[ing] down like waters" and "righteousness like an everflowing stream."

Where was the justice here? Why should I have the luxury of water—while people elsewhere have to walk for hours just to get fresh drinking water? I knew in my heart that it was not a matter of my being favored by God. I knew that God's desire would be for every person to have the same access to clean water, adequate food and clothing, and loving relationships. How can God work through me? What specific responsibility do I have to make things different?

Reflect

~ What does water mean to you?

~ How are you using water? How can you be a better steward?

~ How can you influence others in their use of water?

Pray

Our God, show me ways to make justice roll down like the plentiful water that runs through the pipes in my home. Amen.

– 10 –

Garden of Comfort

Praise God, the Father of our Lord Jesus Christ! The Father is a merciful God, who always gives us comfort. [God] comforts us when we are in trouble, so that we can share that same comfort with others in trouble.

—2 Corinthians 1:3-4

There is a garden that I recall from my childhood. To visit this garden was the highlight of our once a year trip up the center of the state of Florida. We packed our lunch and left Key West early, arriving at Bok Tower somewhere around noon. This tower is located on one of the highest points in Florida, surrounded by acres of lovely gardens.

Edward W. Bok, the man who had the tower built, wanted to leave the world a better place than it was when he was born. The 205-foot Gothic and Art Deco tower houses a 60-bell carillon that sings across the hilltop garden on a daily basis.

The hill, originally covered with scrubby trees and tall pines, was transformed into an informal garden with a reflection pool at the base of the tower. A place of beauty, serenity, and peace, this garden truly reflects the statement that is placed near a path: "I come here to find myself. It's so easy to get lost in the world."

Whether he was aware of it or not, Edward Bok was an agent of God. Creating the tower and the gardens brought God's comfort into a physical realm.

My husband is in the process of building steps down a slope behind our house so that we can easily get into the wooded area. We've already moved the hammock down among the trees. The hammock not only beckons me to rest awhile, but also gives me a feeling of comfort as I look out the kitchen window, seeing the white of the hammock among the green.

We need reminders of God's comfort. We need to keep ourselves alert to take note of these reminders and act on them. If I pass by the window with blind eyes to the hammock, then I've missed that opportunity to pause for a moment and relax in God's care. I've missed the opportunity for comfort. I've not taken advantage of the comfort that God is extending through the work of step building by my husband. We are all extended God's comfort in various ways—ways that we often fail to recognize.

Reflect

~ Who has put forth an effort to extend God's comfort to you? Have you thanked that person?

~ What places offer comfort to you? How can you remind yourself that this comfort comes from God?

~ What can you do to be God's agent and extend comfort to another person?

Pray

God of comfort, thank you for the peace that comes as we rest with you in the troubled times of our lives. Give me opportunities to extend your comfort to others, and help me recognize those opportunities. Amen.

– 11 –

Gardens and the Past

The LORD said: Plant and harvest your crops for six years, but let the land rest during the seventh year.

—Exodus 23:10-11*a*

We expected to find artifacts. After all, we were taking part in an archaeological dig with Elderhostel. The organizing sponsor had already staked out the location. In fact, there had been several groups before us, digging in the dirt an inch at a time. Now we were doing the dirty, sweaty work in southwestern Colorado. Within several feet of us grew dozens of fruit trees, and a creek barely trickled through the gully below.

With the expectation of a child, I sat on the edge of my one square meter of land, brush and trowel in hand. Someone else had excavated the top layers of dirt, and now I was to remove 10 centimeters at a time, recording everything I found. What would I find, and what would it tell us about the past? We knew that the Anasazi culture had lived here, and that they had virtually disappeared. Why had they left? Had they been absorbed into other cultures? There were many mysteries.

We each worked in our own one square meter of land. As we dug, anything of importance was put into bags and labeled with that particular level, block, and unit. Throughout the morning, our group found flakes (from weapon making), pottery chards, bones, and rocks used as tools. There were also large stones, some stacked and some loose. Some of the stacked stones marked the walls of a dwelling. Other stones indicated that there might have been a fireplace at that location because they were charred on one side. There were even ashes inside the small ring of rock.

What might have happened around this ancient fireplace? Certainly there had been cooking, as we found broken animal bones nearby and pottery chards. But what sort of stories were told about their understanding of God and of the world in which they lived? How was love for one another displayed and received? What helped them grow in their faith as they came to know it? What would they have thought about my understanding of God?

As I worked, I suddenly came across a dark object, long and cylindrical. We discovered this to be a part of an irrigation system that was not so ancient! After the ground had lain fallow for many years, and rocks and debris from the nearby cliff had fallen onto the site, the new owners of the land had planted a garden, installing an irrigation system. Now we had evidence of two cultures of mixed times in the same space.

One speculation about the disappearance of the Anasazi is that there was an extended drought, and the people moved to where food was more accessible. After they left, the land lay fallow for many years before being again used for food production in our own time.

The Bible tells us to allow the ground to rest after six years of use. Nature had probably dictated this rest to allow for the restoration of depleted minerals. Nonetheless, this experience made me think about ownership of the land. We will use it only a short time, in the grand scheme of things. In reality, God's loan of the land was as legitimate to the Anasazi as to us. We are to be stewards of God's gifts.

Reflect

~ What has God placed in your care?

~ How can you help others realize that ownership of our material possessions is only temporary?

~ How does God's ownership of the land and all that is in it make a difference in the importance of material possessions?

Pray

God, we are as much indebted to you today as the people of the past. Too often, with our modern conveniences, we forget this. Help me remember that the earth is yours and all that is within it. Amen.

– 12 –

Healing Waters

Jesus answered, "Everyone who drinks this water will get thirsty again. But no one who drinks the water I give will ever be thirsty again. The water I give is like a flowing fountain that gives eternal life."

—John 4:13-14

I lay in bed listening to the sound of water hitting water. We had just installed the fountain pump in our new pond in the garden. The sliding doors were open during this Florida fall evening, and the gentle sound came into our bedroom.

The sound made me recall many other times I've heard the sounds of water. I remembered the sound of rain pelting against the windowpanes in a hurricane. What was coming with the water? Would the roof hold up under the wind? Would a limb from a nearby tree crash through the window and cause the rain to flood our home?

I recalled the rush and roar of waterfalls I've visited. There was the deafening, thundering sound of Niagara Falls and the laughing splash of a tall, slender falls in north Georgia.

I remembered the gurgling water of a creek beside our screened porch in the mountains, and the lazy lapping of water on the side of a canoe on a small river. And I recalled the splash of children and their dog as they jumped from a rock into a lake, and the patter of a grandchild's play at bath time.

I was also reminded of the splashing sound of a man-made stream in the atrium of our local hospital added to create a healing atmosphere. People came from all over the world to experience this atrium garden that enhanced the physical, as well as the emotional, healing of the patients and caregivers alike. When you entered the hospital, you had to walk the full course of the atrium to get to the elevators for the patients' rooms. Passing by this stream was a calming experience.

Our pond became a sacred space in our garden. Often, as I worked around the pond, I recalled that Jesus spoke of himself as the living waters, the waters that gave eternal life. Without water, we die within a week. Water is essential, and likewise God is essential in our lives. Without God our energy is drained and all else ceases to matter.

Reflect

~ When have you had dry spells? What brought about relief?

~ How many water faucets do you have? How can turning on a faucet remind you of the living waters that Christ offered?

~ What uses of water are essential in our lives? How do they relate to the essence of Christ?

Pray

God, I welcome the healing waters of your love. Refresh my soul with the healing waters that Jesus offered. Amen.

– 13 –

Beyond My Garden

Then the people will ask, "LORD, when did we fail to help you when you were hungry or thirsty or a stranger or naked or sick or in jail?" The king will say to them, "Whenever you failed to help any of my people, no matter how unimportant they seemed, you failed to do it for me."

—Matthew 25:44-45

Our subdivision has covenants that regulate certain things about our houses and our yards. Covenants help people maintain the quality of a neighborhood, but at times we wish that they were not there. I regret that I can't hang my sheets out on a clothesline in my garden. It was a hassle to go before the architectural board when we wanted to build a deck. At other times, I've been appreciative of the covenants, and I knew about them when we moved into the neighborhood.

Our daughter lives in a subdivision where the front yards are cared for by the maintenance crew that her homeowners' association hires. Her backyard is an enclosed area that is her responsibility. When some of her neighbors added plants to their front yards, the homeowners' association informed them that they must be dug up because the added plants kept the yards from being uniform.

There is something within us that wants to be in control. We want to decide what happens to us. This causes us to resist, and even to resent, events and people who interrupt the "ideal" direction that we have set for our lives. We create our own worlds, our own gardens. And we are resentful when we are forced to venture beyond our garden gates or when something that we haven't planned ventures into our gardens.

Seeing a homeless person in our neighborhood disturbs us. We know, intellectually, that God cares for homeless people as much as for us. But it still disturbs us! We know that they must be cared for by someone, somewhere. But we say:

Not in my neighborhood! Not in my world!

Don't bring the cares of the world to my front door!

Don't bring the immigrants to my shores!

Don't remind me that there are those for whom I should care!

Don't upset my apple cart!

The world that we create for ourselves when we have that attitude is a false world. The real world is glossed over—often glossed over with a checkbook. We soothe our conscience by giving a donation, but refuse to become a part of the world where others live. We create our own little fishbowl, and as we look through the distorted glass, we see the world as we want to see it. We forget that Jesus said, "If you did it (or didn't do it) to these, then you did (or didn't do) it to me." We would never believe that we would ignore the needs of our beloved Christ. But, sadly, we do.

Abiding by the covenants in my subdivision is a must. But no one makes me ignore those who live outside my subdivision. That happens when I resist Christ's call. A sacred space is not always what we envision in our gardens. God's sacred places are often in the slums or in the prisons, because that is where God can be most active. That is where we can, and must, really get our hands in the dirt!

Reflect

~ How have you created a comfortable world that ignores others?

~ What do you need to change in your life in order to see the world as it really is?

~ What specific thing can you do to follow Christ's call to treat others as you would treat him?

Pray

Help me look beyond my own garden, Lord. Open my eyes to the real world. Amen.

– 14 –

Pictures of the Past

Such a large crowd of witnesses is all around us! So we must get rid of everything that slows us down, especially the sin that just won't let go. And we must be determined to run the race that is ahead of us.

—Hebrews 12:1

Each year I carefully pull up milkweed seedlings that sprout in my lawn and transfer them into my garden. The milkweed is a primary attraction for monarch butterflies. The monarch lays her eggs on the plant, and then the caterpillar dines on the leaves as it grows. The seeds of the plant are attached to cotton-like fiber and, when released, drift with the wind, catching in the lawn.

I received my first seeds from Joy, a neighbor gardener in Florida, about ten years ago. She was given the seeds by a friend before she moved from the east to the west coast of the state, to start her butterfly garden. Later, when her friend died, Joy realized that the seeds she had received were like an embodiment of her friend. She told the friend's daughter, "The seeds I planted are still blooming, and seeds from those plants have been shared with others. And, in a way, the blooms are people who have gone."

I have many plants in my garden that are pictures of the past, pictures of times with friends and relatives, both living and dead. My father, who died twenty-three years ago, gave me several amaryllis bulbs. They have bloomed in five of my gardens now. Although I don't have the same irises that were in my mother-in-law's garden, I do remember her when I plant another iris in my garden. On my last move I brought a dozen or so daylilies with me that a former neighbor and I had ordered together and tended in our gardens. I have additional daylilies and irises that a gardening friend in my Sunday school class shared with me.

Around my house are several azaleas, a hydrangea bush, and a wisteria that I am training into a tree. These are transplants from my cousin's garden. I recently purchased a trellis for a Carolina jasmine that came from the garden of Karen, a friend we made in Florida. Her vine had grown into a canopy over a small terrace outside her dining room window. My small start soon covered the fence between my garden and my neighbor's, and I brought a bit of it to Georgia. In the meantime, Karen moved from Florida to Kansas City to Canton, Ohio. Now she has moved about twenty miles from where I live, and I dug up a bit of the plant and gave it back to her!

Outside my study window I am watching an Easter lily as it bursts into bloom, a plant that graced the altar of our church last year in memory of our parents. Next year, two additional lilies will bloom. These also came from our church, having been given in honor of our grandchildren.

I carefully water a climbing rose and a tree rose, each given to me by our daughter and son. The massive Cherokee rose covering my bedroom window was rooted in a vase in my daughter's kitchen window, and I also have daisy blooms and spreading "hen and chicks" that came from my son's garden.

How sacred is my garden! In it I am reminded of so many friends and relatives. Some have gone on to other gardens, and some have their own gardens on earth. But each makes my garden sacred because their relationship encourages me in the faith!

Reflect

~ What in your garden bears witness to your friends, both present and past?

~ What from your garden can you share with others, continuing that witness to friendship?

~ What else in your garden makes it a sacred place?

Pray

Many of the plants in my garden witness to the wonderful friendships and relationships I've had in my life. God, I thank you for the opportunity to know these people. Amen.

My Garden Holds Hidden Joys

– 15 –

Birds, Great and Small

But those who trust the LORD will find new strength. They will be strong like eagles soaring upward on wings; they will walk and run without getting tired.

—Isaiah 40:31

Birds that visit my garden are one of the pluses in life. I have a friend who has a set of binoculars in every room of her house that overlooks her garden. Sometimes she spends time simply sitting and observing the birds, and at other times she watches them in passing.

From our garden in Florida, we often saw an eagle soaring high above. Rather than expending all its energy flapping its wings, this bird has learned to use the wind currents to its advantage as it circles, looking for prey.

In our Georgia garden, we have a large variety of birds. Some of the most frequent visitors are the bright yellow goldfinches. They flock around the thistle feeder hanging upside down on the perches and eating from the holes in the feeders that are strategically placed below the perches.

Beside the thistle feeder we planted a dogwood tree, and the goldfinches use the branches as a waiting area when there are more birds than perches. Although these goldfinches are very light in weight, occasionally one will land on a small limb that doesn't support its weight. When the finch rises out of the fall, with complete confidence in its wings, I sometimes hear it singing. This reminds me of these lines by Victor Hugo:

Be like the bird, who / halting on his flight / on limb too slight, / feels it give way beneath him, / yet sings, / knowing he has wings.

Whether we have the strength of an eagle or the simple power of a goldfinch, we too can be confident that God will help us rise above every fall. God does not place pitfalls in our way, but God does give us wings to come out of them, loving us all the while.

Reflect

~ When have you felt as small as a goldfinch? Or as powerful as an eagle?

~ Where has God helped you or someone else rise above a fall?

~ How can you express your joy for God's help even in the midst of a fall?

Pray

My God, you created the birds that frequent my garden. Show me the lessons that they teach, even when I'm least open to learning them. Amen.

– 16 –

Garden Rock

Anyone who hears and obeys these teachings of mine is like a wise person who built a house on solid rock. Rain poured down, rivers flooded, and winds beat against that house. But it did not fall, because it was built on solid rock. Anyone who hears my teachings and doesn't obey them is like a foolish person who built a house on sand. The rain poured down, the rivers flooded, and the winds blew and beat against that house. Finally, it fell with a crash.

—Matthew 7:24-27

I stood beside the house, spade in hand, with a row of azalea plants ready to be put into the ground. They would make a great display of color in the spring! I could already visualize it. First I pushed aside the pine straw mulch that the builder's workers had spread around the foundation. Then I placed my spade on top of the soil and applied pressure with my foot. The blade went into the ground about two inches and then balked. Ah, I thought, one of those rocks that I'd dug out of other places where I'd planted. So I simply moved the shovel over a few inches and tried again. Again the blade hit rock. And again and again and again.

Now I got down close to my work and began pushing the few inches of dirt aside. To my surprise, I kept uncovering rock. The exposed rock stretched from near the foundation of our house to the grass, and from under the air conditioner to near the corner of the house. At that point, the rock did drop off so that I had enough dirt to plant an azalea.

Now what was I to do with this boulder of a rock? Obviously the landscaper had decided to leave it rather than move it, though I would like to have had it dug up and placed on top of the ground. I could simply place pine straw over it and leave the space bare without plants.

As I looked at the rock, I was reminded of Jesus' parable about the house built on the rock and the house built on sand. I decided to leave the top of this boulder exposed in the midst of my foundation plantings to remind me that I must always build my house, my life, and my dreams on the firm foundation of Christ.

Reflect

~ What are the foundations of your faith? How do they affect your life?

~ When have you found a strength that seemed to be hidden?

~ What thwarted places in your life can be turned into reminders of God's strength?

Pray

Give me wisdom, God, to expose the strength that you lay before me. Let the hard places become reminders of your strength. Amen.

– 17 –

Ants Will Be Ants

You lazy people can learn by watching an anthill. Ants don't have leaders, but they store up food during harvest season. How long will you lie there doing nothing at all? When are you going to get up and stop sleeping? Sleep a little. Doze a little. Fold your hands and twiddle your thumbs. Suddenly, everything is gone, as though it had been taken by an armed robber.

—Proverbs 6:6-11

It was mid-spring, and I cherished the seedling alyssum plants by my back door. I had bought one plant the year before, and now in the spot I'd planted it, I found a dozen or so seedlings. As small as they were, they were already beginning to show their white cushion of blooms. This was the day to move them, spacing them out along the edge of the bed so that they would have room to grow and spread their joy.

As I lifted the first plant, ants swarmed out of the disturbed dirt. Little black bodies with wiggling legs moved up my hand-spade and onto my garden gloves. No time for reflection now! I dropped the spade and seedling and brushed the ants off as quickly as I could. I knew all too well the hours of itching that each little bite would cause. Those ants may be small, but their bites are fierce.

My reflection came later as I wrote in my journal. I remembered that the author of Proverbs had something to say about learning a lesson from the ants. Was the author calling me lazy? Did he know that I sometimes play a game of cards on the computer instead of sticking to my work? Did the author realize just how close to home these statements would come?

Alas, my sins had found me out through my reflections. I—the world's best procrastinator—needed to learn a lesson here. There is such a thing as knowing your capability and being able to work well, right up to a deadline. But there is also a time of reckoning. Perhaps the restless sleep that I sometimes experience as a deadline approaches could be avoided if I did not put things off until the last minute. I must take seriously the challenge to be a better steward of my time.

I was able to finish transplanting the alyssum, a plant at a time. Now, each time I see the tiny white blooms, I recall the lesson that the author of Proverbs gave me. Don't wait for someone to tell you what to do! Wade in there and get busy. Your destiny is in your own hands. If you sleep, everything will be gone, taken away without your knowledge.

Reflect

~ What is keeping you from the work that God calls you to?

~ What habits can you change to better carry out your responsibilities?

~ How can you meet the challenge to readjust your life to become a better steward of your time?

Pray

God of the ants and God of my time, help me learn the lessons taught by your tiny creatures. Help me stick to my tasks, even when I'd rather be doing something else. Amen.

– 18 –

Johnny-Jump-ups

Plant your seeds early in the morning and keep working in the field until dark. Who knows? Your work might pay off, and your seeds might produce.

—Ecclesiastes 11:6

I looked out my front door one morning this spring, and in the corner of the lawn I saw a bright spot of yellow. Surely not a dandelion, I thought. Upon closer examination, I recognized the plant as a little Johnny-jump-up, like the ones I had planted near the sidewalk the previous year. They are prolific bloomers, and evidently the rainwater from the downspout had washed their seeds into the lawn. But this one was all the way across the lawn near the street.

I could not let this bright spot of color be mowed down with the first cutting of the lawn. Gently, I pierced the ground with my narrow digger, loosening the roots, and moved it into the bedding area, beneath the birdbath. A few days later, I discovered more Johnny Jump-ups in our lawn. They too were gently uprooted and moved to safer ground.

This experience reminded me of an incident several years ago when I was in a small-group Bible study. As we shared stories about people who had been instrumental in our spiritual growth, one of the men recalled something I had said several years before—an incident I had completely forgotten. It was an awakening experience to have him recall that as a turning point in his faith, when I could hardly remember it.

I thought of the various seeds that I've thrown into a garbage bag for curb pickup. Those seeds ended up in a landfill somewhere, and perhaps some of them even produced flowers. There is no way of knowing just how far and wide my seeds have spread.

We never know when or where seeds of faith will be sown. Most often we will be unaware of the seeds we are scattering among those we know or encounter. Like the seeds I've discarded with dead flowers, we may never know the outcome or the persons who benefit from our seeds of faith. We can, and do, make a difference, either positively or negatively, in the lives of others. So we must tune ourselves to those opportunities and strive to make them positive.

The hidden joy of a Johnny-jump-up reminds me of how I share faith in unrecognized ways.

Reflect

~ Who has made a difference in your faith quest? Have you told that person?

~ When have you consciously shared some aspect of your faith with another person?

~ Where can you spread seeds of faith?

Pray

My God, help me be aware of the many opportunities to share your love. Keep me conscious of all the things I say and do, since they may be seeds for someone else's soul. Amen.

– 19 –

Blackberries, Precious Treasures

Where then is wisdom? It is hidden from human eyes and even from birds. God is the only one who knows the way to wisdom.

—Job 28:21, 23

O n the small hill behind my house I constantly fight blackberry bushes. This is not a convenient place for these prickly vines to rise up from the ground. It is against the covenant of our homeowner's association. We must keep the hill clean cut or planted with acceptable vegetation. This is one occasion where I recognize the importance of conforming in the minor things to keep peace. When I drive past houses with tall weeds in the yards, I also remember why we purchased a house in a neighborhood with a covenant agreement.

However, every July I certainly appreciate the blackberry bushes along the roadsides and on abandoned property. Early in the morning, while it is still cool, I don my old jeans and a long-sleeved shirt, grab a couple of buckets, and head for the blackberry patch. Before anyone else in the household is awake, I'm usually back with my buckets full and my clothing wet with sweat. I also return with a deeper soul.

I find so many hidden treasures of truth and wisdom in blackberry picking. The vines remind me of Christ's suffering for us. The spreading roots remind me that no matter how often Christ's message is cut off, it will continue to spread from the roots. The white blossoms signal hope of the coming harvest. Blackberry winter, the cold spell that sets the fruit, reminds me that the adversities that come our way can make us stronger. The seeds that sometime lodge between my teeth remind me of the seeds of faith that I need to plant in others. And the juice reminds me of Christ's blood, shed for us.

But even more important than these hidden treasures, I find blackberry picking an opportunity to grow my soul by simply being with God. I've discovered this since no one else in my family has ever cared to share the joys of blackberry picking with me! And so when I go early and spend time alone in the wilds of the blackberry patch, I return sweaty, scratched, and tired. But I also come away with a better sense of who I am and a better sense of who God is.

The covenants of my neighborhood may keep the blackberry bushes out of my garden, but they can't keep the blackberry lessons out of my soul.

Reflect

~ What adversities in your life have made you stronger?

~ How do you relate to the other metaphors mentioned, even if blackberry picking is not a passion of yours?

~ What experiences in nature help to grow your soul?

Pray

God of the briar patch as well as the cultivated garden, I thank you for the opportunities to grow my soul. I will seek you in the blackberry patches of my life as well as in the rose gardens. Amen.

– 20 –

Seasons Here and Seasons There

Then every tree in the forest will sing joyful songs to the LORD.

—Psalm 96:12

When we moved to Florida fifteen years ago, people asked if we would miss the changing seasons. I knew from my previous years in Florida—and soon rediscovered—that Florida has many more seasons than other states. They are just more subtle. Each time we experienced the orange canopy of blooms of the poinciana trees or when the fruit developed on our star fruit tree, we knew we were in a different season.

When we moved back to four-season country two years ago, I remembered what I liked about my seasonal gardens. I agree with the psalmist: The trees do sing joyful songs to the Lord. During each season, the trees in my garden sing a distinctively different song from the previous one, and each season has its own charm.

In summertime the trees sing a song of the fullness of life. They praise God with the wind blowing through their branches and the rain prancing on their leaves. They praise God for the opportunity to house nesting birds and for the canopy of shade they can provide on hot summer days.

In the fall the trees sing with their vibrant colors. The oranges and yellows and reds stand out in contrast to the patches of evergreens. And then as the season wears on, their leaves dance to the song of wind through their branches, whirling from the limbs and skipping across the lawns.

Even after the last leaf has fallen, the trees find joy in singing throughout the winter. Now they expose their various textured trunks, and their bare limbs reach to God's heavens above. Even when their usual song is hushed by a blanket of snow, they continue to whisper joy for God's creation.

Then spring comes around once more, and the trees can no longer contain themselves but burst forth in a new birth. Surely, we think, God has made a wonderful world! Despite the pollution, dirt, and hatred that we people have spread across the world, each spring the trees bring a new promise. Their song is one of hope, of God making something new from what appears to be dead.

Seasons come and go, and we sometimes fail to listen to each new song. But the trees of my garden remind me that God is still in control, and I will sing songs of joy and thanksgiving with each oak and pine, each maple and hickory, each dogwood and apple.

Reflect

~ Which season is your favorite? How do you see God in it?

~ How can you find a joy in seasons that depress you?

~ In what other ways do the trees speak to you of God?

Pray

Joyfully I sing with the trees, O God. I sing of the joy of creation. I sing for joy at the way you created me as a distinct individual. Amen.

My Garden Provides Lessons for Life

– 21 –

Holy Leisure with Pain

We gladly suffer, because we know that suffering helps us to endure. And endurance builds character, which gives us hope that will never disappoint us. All of this happens because God has given us the Holy Spirit, who fills our hearts with his love.

—Romans 5:3-5

I awoke with the dawning light, my favorite time to awaken, when the day is new and unused. I looked around my sunny bedroom and thought of all I planned to do that day. After a good stretch, I threw my feet over the side of the bed and stood up. But as I took my first steps, the pain of my sore muscles made me temporarily forget my plans for the day! The muscles were not accustomed to the workout they had received in my garden.

I was reminded of the women I met when I was in Mozambique the previous year. All their work was done on mats on the ground instead of on tables or counters. Their muscles were accustomed to bending and stooping, but they were wise about their bending. Instead of bending their backs, they bent from their hips with their knees slightly bent and backs straight. A few days later, when I gardened again, I tried their technique. To my joy, I discovered that this produced much less soreness the next day.

Many different kinds of suffering come into our lives—physical suffering, emotional suffering, and even suffering through stress. In no way do I believe that God sends this suffering, but I do believe that God uses all of the suffering in our lives to bring about spiritual growth.

God desires for all people to live happy, healthy lives. But God also gave us individual choice, and sometimes our choices—or those of other people—have a negative impact on our lives, bringing about suffering in one form or another.

But if we allow God's Holy Spirit to work with us through the suffering, then as Paul said, we will build character and strength that brings about hope in the end.

Reflect

~ What suffering have you endured that has ultimately resulted in hope?

~ Do you think of God weeping with you when you suffer?

~ How does Jesus' human suffering offer us comfort?

Pray

God, because you suffered in a human form, help me realize that you also understand my own suffering. Draw me closer to you and give me hope that you will bring something good from my suffering. Amen.

– 22 –

Oak Tree Lessons

The kingdom of heaven is like what happens when a farmer plants a mustard seed in a field. Although it is the smallest of all seeds, it grows larger than any garden plant and becomes a tree. Birds even come and nest on its branches.

—Matthew 13:31-32

Growing up in the South, I was always puzzled by this verse. My knowledge of mustard seeds was of garden greens instead of a tree, but I learned that some strains of the mustard plant do grow large enough to hold a bird.

If Jesus were here today, he might have used an oak tree that stood beside one of my gardens as an example. That oak tree towered above all other trees in the vicinity, but, alas, it died. When the ground was disturbed for the foundation of our new home, dirt was pushed around the base of the tree. The dirt cut off the air source at the base of the tree, resulting in damage that was beyond repair.

After hiring someone to cut the tree down, my husband began splitting the logs that would later provide fuel for our wood furnace. As I helped him stack the wood, I reflected on the massive oak tree.

The oak had begun as a very small acorn many years earlier. Very much like our faith, it began as a seedling, not much longer than my finger. Each year of growth brought another ring to its trunk. Each experience of my life brings another layer to my faith. At all stages of the tree's growth, it was still an oak. The same is true with my faith, and with the faith of any other person. No matter where we are in our spiritual growth, our faith is a part of the kingdom of heaven.

The oak was useful to many during the years of growth. It held the bank of dirt beside a rushing stream. It provided food for squirrels and shade and shelter for humans and animals alike. Through all these services, it continued to grow and mature. Likewise, my faith must reach out to others if it is to grow. As faith is strengthened through service, the kingdom of heaven comes closer to fulfillment.

Beginning as a small seed, oaks and faith alike grow to maturity. The oak's final fate was not in its dying. It continued to give by providing fuel and warmth in winter months. As the trunk rotted, it gave nourishment back to the earth. The fulfillment of the kingdom of heaven may not come in our lifetime, but our growing faith helps bring it about. Each time we give of ourselves in service, we are a part of the kingdom that is here and now.

Reflect

~ How has your faith grown in the past year? In the past month?

~ Where do you see the kingdom of heaven around you?

~ What are you doing to help bring about the kingdom?

Pray

Our God, show me ways you need each of us to help bring the kingdom of Heaven to fulfillment. Show me ways I can expand my faith through service for the kingdom. Amen.

– 23 –

Remembering Joys

Don't worry about tomorrow. It will take care of itself. You have enough to worry about today.

—Matthew 6:34

Darkness began to creep upon me. I had worked in the garden far later than I intended. But the joy of digging in the dirt, the joy of watching for new growth, and the joy of creating a holy place had taken over! I could not bring myself to quit as long as there was any daylight left.

The next morning as I awoke, the thought came to me—What if, in the morning, I found myself paralyzed, never again able to dig my hands in the dirt or hold a watering hose? What would be my thoughts about the last time I had gardened? Did I appreciate yesterday's work at its fullest?

Do we ever fully appreciate the "last time" of any experience until we must look back on it as the last? Think of the last meal that the disciples had with Jesus. Although it was the Passover, it could have felt a little ordinary at the time. They were aware that Jesus was in some danger. Frequently, the officials had tried to trip him up with leading questions. But it is likely that the full impact of that meal did not hit them until after his death and they recognized it as their last meal together. No wonder they established a way of remembering that event by eating together when they met. This eventually became our Eucharist.

We are often so involved with our busyness that we let special opportunities pass us by. We see incidents as routine, occasions as preliminary to something greater, and events as accomplishments. We fill our calendar and then complain that we have no time. We pride ourselves at being overcommitted. We have forgotten how to live for the moment. We continually anticipate the future while missing the joy of the present.

Jesus recognized this. His statement about fretting over tomorrow can be applied to our schedules as well as our food. Jesus would have us live each day to its fullest, to simply appreciate each moment as it comes. Tomorrow will take care of itself!

Reflect

~ When you list all of your activities and boast about your busyness, are you simply building up your own ego?

~ What can you put aside for the future so that you can enjoy today?

~ How can you discern just what is important in your life and what should be postponed—perhaps never to be brought up again?

Pray

God, give me a self-esteem that is not dependent on my busyness. Help me use every opportunity to live in the joy of the moment and to pass this joy on to others. Amen.

– 24 –

Thumbs, Both Green and Brown

There are different kinds of spiritual gifts, but they all come from the same Spirit. There are different ways to serve the same LORD, and we can each do different things. Yet the same God works in all of us and helps us in everything we do.

—1 Corinthians 12:4-6

Yqou certainly have a green thumb," she commented. "Mine is totally brown."

My neighbor was admiring my cascading Cherokee rose. Hundreds of pinkish white blossoms spilled across our bedroom window, the result of a single eight-inch slip pulled from a bush growing wild along the road. Our daughter had broken off the branch two years before and put it in water on her windowsill. When the blooms faded, she left it there because the leaves were still fresh. Soon she noticed roots forming at the broken end of the branch, and at the end of the summer she gave it to me to plant in the yard of our new home.

The cutting barely had time to sink its roots into the ground before the first frost, but it survived the winter and put on new growth in the spring. The first summer the rosebush outgrew the trellis I had put up and spilled over onto the lawn, but did not bloom. Now, in its second spring, the bush was eight feet tall and had a mass of blooms. I had only provided soil and water during dry seasons. How could I take credit for the mass of glory? But my neighbor insisted that my daughter and I both had a green thumb, a gift from God.

Having worked on staff in many churches, I have come to realize that God endowed each of us with special gifts or abilities. Some are obvious and some more subtle, but each is special. The secret to joy in service is to find that passion or gift that God gave you, and to cultivate and use it.

One year, as I taught a sixth-grade class, we talked about the gifts that God has given each of us. I asked the class members to draw a picture or write a paragraph about a special ability that God had given them. One boy came up to me cautiously and said, "God didn't give me anything." I asked what subject in school he liked and did well in. His answer was math. I smiled and told him that God hadn't given me the gift of math, but if he did well in that subject, he could be sure that it was a gift from God. He sat at the table and enjoyed making a display of math problems.

Some of us have gifts of obvious things such as painting or writing or acting or making significant speeches. Others have gifts in sports or in music. There are gifts of hospitality, of decorating, and even of map reading. Our caring ministries can use people with gifts of listening, of cooking, and of discernment. To bring about God's kingdom, each of our gifts is important.

I acknowledged the affirmation of my gift of a green thumb. But I also realize that I am endowed with many gifts, just as my neighbor is and just as you are too.

Reflect

~ What gifts from God do you have?

~ How are you using them, and in what additional ways can you use them?

~ Think about people you know who do not have obvious gifts. What subtle gifts do they have? How can you affirm their giftedness?

Pray

My God, I thank you for the gifts that I am using. Help me find additional ways to use these gifts, and also to discover other gifts that have not been developed. By using your gifts, I want to help bring about your kingdom. Amen.

– 25 –

God's Diverse World

Jesus prayed: "May they be brought to complete unity to let the world know that you sent me and have loved them even as you have loved me."

—John 17:23 NIV

I looked out my kitchen window into my garden. Stalks of iris stood side by side with pink and purple blooms. These were large flowers, the bearded type. I found pleasure in these flowers. As I observed the colors, however, I recalled the time in my childhood when I was told that pink and purple did not go together. Neither did yellow and orange, I was told. According to the fashions of the day, these colors were not acceptable to wear together. I never understood that, because in nature God put them side by side. I even found them together on the same flowers.

I enjoy the diversity in my garden. I will put herbs among my roses, and pansies with the holly. My father and mother could never garden together. Mother liked her garden to have everything together according to its variety. My father's garden plans usually started out that way, but when he had an extra plant or seed at the end of a row, he would put it at some other location rather than discard it or crowd the existing rows. Dad had garden peas growing in beds along the sidewalk because he had extra seeds and ran out of space. He had pumpkins that climbed a tree amid the turnips. And the carrots and beets thrust their roots into the ground together.

Our son enjoys diverse gardening too. His garden plot isn't much larger than a good-sized pantry, but he has raspberries, strawberries, tomatoes, lettuce, broccoli, carrots, and beans. His peas climb the fence, and grapes hang from a canopy overhead. It is an adventure in discovery to walk through his garden!

God's world is made up of diversity. There is diversity in people as well as in nature. We are diverse in our looks, in our interests, in our talents and gifts, and even in our beliefs. But, when it comes to our beliefs, we often forget that God loves diversity. Christians have fought "holy wars" over beliefs. We have created enemies out of fellow Christians. (What is it that Christ said about loving our enemies? Have we forgotten this?) We have split congregations and turned people away from our churches because they see us as hypocrites. We have spent money and time on arguments over small matters. Such money and time could better be spent feeding and housing the poor. This is the witness that Christ gave.

Christ prayed for our unity in the midst of diversity. Often we equate unity with uniformity. But we cannot see new perspectives if we insist on uniformity. With uniformity we do not learn from others, and we lose our ability to grow in world community.

Diversity reflects God's love as light reflects from the diverse facets of a diamond. Each facet of a diamond faces the world in a different manner and gathers the light in a different way, reflecting that light brilliantly. Yet there is unity in the facets of a diamond. It takes all of the facets to bring out the radiance of the stone. And there must be light, for the diamond cannot shine in darkness. The same is true with our souls. We must become diverse and many-faceted, and we must expose ourselves to the Source of all light. But we must also unite with others to reflect God's light to the world.

Reflect

~ When have you become hung up on uniformity and forgotten to appreciate diversity?

~ What minor matters has your faith community spent energy and money on that could have been used to better Christ's church?

~ How can you use diversity to grow your soul?

Pray

God of us all, bring us together to praise and work for you. Give me the courage to stand up for all, no matter how different they are from me and from my beliefs. Amen.

– 26 –

Focusing

Show me your ways, O LORD, teach me your paths; guide me in your truth and teach me, for you are God my Savior, and my hope is in you all day long.

—Psalm 25:4-5 NIV

Each spring, I organize my gardening time, putting reminders on my calendar when certain plants need fertilizer or when certain shrubs need pruning. I develop many far-out dreams of what to do with my garden and how to organize my gardening time. Those dreams stimulate excitement, and I want to go in all directions and accomplish too many things at once.

Once I begin working in the garden, I have difficulty focusing on and pulling in the reins of my runaway dreams about what I can reasonably accomplish. I begin clipping back some shrubs, and a stray weed beckons me. I may pull a strand of grass that has crept into the flowerbed, and then see a misplaced seedling in the lawn. As I move the seedling, I realize that the tomatoes need watering. Before I know it my gardening time is gone, and I've jumped from one job to another, never accomplishing what I started out to do.

But isn't that the way with much of life? We can't concentrate on one area because we keep jumping to something else. We see so many needs that we spread ourselves too thin and thus aren't effective in any area. Similarly, when I am low on fertilizer, I try to spread it out to cover the entire garden. The end result is many mediocre plants, none of them blooming.

Many books have been written about discovering your spiritual gifts. But trying to determine where God wants us to work can be confusing. Perhaps that's why we sometimes spread ourselves too thin. But if you have a real passion for something, then that is very likely where your gifts and your ministry lie. However, if you continue to flounder with finding a direction, just jump in and try something. Often we don't know whether a particular ministry is right until we've tried it out.

But the important thing is to be engaged in God's ministry in some way. If all of my dreams for my garden are only on paper, I'll never see any fruits. Even when I jump from one thing to another, I'm at least trying. But it is also important that I concentrate on one area to accomplish what I set out to do there. Then I can make the jump to something else if it's not my passion.

Reflect

~ What ministries have you tried in or beyond your church?

~ Where is your passion in ministry? What do you enjoy doing?

~ How can you concentrate on your ministry and thus be more effective?

Pray

There are so many needs and areas where I feel connected, Lord. You gave me special gifts. Help me use those gifts in the way that I can be most effective. Amen.

– 27 –

New Garden Gloves

You are the one who put me together inside my mother's body, and I praise you because of the wonderful way you created me. Everything you do is marvelous! Of this I have no doubt.

—Psalm 139:13-14

Anyone who has shopped for garden gloves knows how difficult finding the right ones can be. The gloves must fit well; they must be flexible; and they must stand up under heavy use, both in and out of water.

When I first began gardening, the only gloves I could find were all made from a heavy canvas that would hardly bend. Thankfully, manufacturers have come up with better materials and better fits. I was grateful when they began making tighter fitting gloves of cotton fabric. They wore out quickly, but at least they were inexpensive. Now you can find gloves that are made of blends or leather or plastic or even rubberized fabric—all more flexible. The materials must fit your needs as a gardener as well as your personal preference.

It is important that garden gloves fit well. If they are too large, they become more of a hindrance than help. They may fit in length, from the wrist to the tips of your fingers, but if the fingers aren't snug fitting you'll never be able to transplant seedlings or grasp small weeds.

It is a joy to find garden gloves that fit and are flexible

for my work. Then I know that someone cares about me and about my gardening.

God made each of us different. Before we were born, God put us together in our mother's womb, and each one of us is unique. We each have our own physical as well as spiritual DNA. This makes us special to God, and unique in our relationship with God. Just as there are a variety of garden gloves, there are many spiritual practices, such as meditation, journaling, music, and poetry. You may find one more helpful than another in growing your soul. Because someone else embraces a certain practice does not mean it will be right for you. Unless we try on different sizes of spiritual gloves, unless we work with them for a while, we cannot know just what fits us properly.

And, just as we must always be on the lookout for those new styles of garden gloves, it is important to continually try new ways to grow our souls.

Reflect

~ What special needs does your soul DNA have for growth?

~ What are some things you might try that you haven't tried before?

~ What section of the Bible can you center on that you haven't used recently?

Pray

You made me special, God, and I must find my special way to grow my soul. Give me guidance, and put in me a desire to approach you in a variety of ways. Amen.

My Garden Gives Sabbath Time

– 28 –

Lessons from a Hummingbird

Then Jesus said, "Let's go to a place where we can be alone and get some rest."

—Mark 6:31*b*

We have two types of hummingbird feeders in our garden. One is a mobile, a lovely hanging sculpture with three oval bottles. On the same pole I have also placed a hanging basket of fuchsia. The other is a simple, old-fashioned feeder.

The hummers hover among the fuchsia blooms and mobile feeder, sipping nectar as they go about their way. They take nourishment in flight with tiny wings flapping about sixty-five times a second. Sometimes I think they expend more energy furiously flapping their wings than they take in with their occasional sip from the fuchsia and feeding bottles.

Then I notice that these tiny birds come to rest at the old-fashioned feeder. Here they have a perch on which to rest while they fill themselves with the nourishment they need. Here they may drink to their heart's content without expending their much-needed energy.

How much we are like the little hummingbird. We rush through our lives, sipping the essence of God's love here and there throughout the day. And it is good and nourishes us. But there comes a time during our flights when we must pause and drink our fill. Our hunger is too great to be completely filled on the run—or in flight, whatever the case may be.

How wonderful to have Christ invite us into a place where we can be alone with him! Imagine the opportunity to sit with Jesus and talk about the important things, drinking in his presence and wisdom.

Reflect

~ What opportunities of spiritual nourishment do you take advantage of throughout each day?

~ Do you burn "soul energy" faster than you can replace it on the run?

~ When do you make a time away to simply spend with God?

Pray

O God, our nourishment, I thank you for the opportunities to get "soul energy" on the run. Help me also take advantage of quiet, restful times that are so necessary for replenishing myself. Amen.

– 29 –

Fog in the Garden

If you are tired from carrying heavy burdens, come to me and I will give you rest.

—Matthew 11:28

There is fog in my garden today, so thick I can hardly see the roof of my neighbor's house. There's something protective about fog, as long as I don't have to travel in it. Fog surrounds me and keeps distractions out. I'm centered—just God and me here in the garden.

Fog mutes the rough lines of the landscape. Things are not so distinct. Can the metaphor of fog be applied to my spiritual life? You may consider fog as a hindrance, causing accidents on the highway and blocking our view of the truth. But I prefer to see fog in a positive sense. Looking at a situation through the fog requires me to ask questions. Is it really there? Do I really see what I think I see, or is it a delusion? Can I trust what someone else is telling me about the situation since that person is also standing beside me and looking through the fog?

The fog of our spiritual life requires us to move closer to answer these questions. We must enter into the fog itself, go beyond the boundaries of comfort, and encounter all that is out there. But we are often afraid of doing this since it is risky, and we don't know what it will bring. Moving closer to God means opening ourselves to

God to be used, acknowledging that God knows all about us, and moving to an intimate relationship with our Creator. Sometimes we'd rather observe God safely from a distance, shrouded in the mystery of the fog.

The morning fog hides the brilliant purple flowers growing beneath the trees in the woods behind my house. I would miss the joy of those blossoms if I remained in the fog, never moving closer to the plants. The same is true when I keep God at a distance, shrouded in the fog. But if I move closer, the fog brings a Sabbath, a brilliance beyond anticipation!

Reflect

~ What questions do you encounter in the fog of your spiritual life? Do you recognize the freedom to pursue the answers yourself?

~ What sort of distractions keep you from centering on God?

~ What are you afraid of revealing to God? When have you found joy by releasing your fears to God?

Pray

Come, Holy Spirit. Swirl around me and beacon me closer to the peace of Sabbath in the fog. Fill me with brilliant anticipation, even as I encounter questions. Free me from my fear so that I may come near for a closer view. Amen.

– 30 –

Peaceful Garden

I give you peace, the kind of peace that only I can give. It isn't like the peace that this world can give. So don't be worried or afraid.

—John 14:27

In the cold of the winter, I like to thumb through gardening magazines. One of my favorites has no advertisements, only lovely photographs and interesting articles. Surprisingly, the cost of the magazine is little more than those with ads, but there are fewer pages. This magazine also features gardens of everyday people instead of famous gardens cultivated by a hired staff. It gives me hope that I can also create a beautiful and peaceful garden of my own.

My garden is in a continual state of becoming. There is always something else I'd like to do to the garden to improve it—another plant to add or move, mulch to put down, a step or walk to add, or a bed to raise. These projects bring excitement and a happy heart. As long as I don't dwell on instant accomplishment, the plans can bring peace to my soul.

My garden can also bring peace to my soul when I have a sad heart. I find peace in the physical work needed to bring about that little plot of paradise. Sometimes I find peace by simply standing at the kitchen window and gazing into the garden. We recently moved our hammock from the sunny deck into the shade of the woods beyond the garden. Even when I don't have the opportunity to walk out into the garden, simply seeing that white hammock among the green of the woods can bring peace.

I've discovered that the peacefulness of the garden often reflects the attitude that I bring with me. If I come to my garden with a frenzied need for accomplishment, then the gardening chores become frustrating. But if I come to my garden with an attitude of joyful anticipation, then the work brings peace.

Sometimes, when I'm short on time, it's better that I put off a job until a less stressful day. On those occasions, I simply enjoy my garden during the short time I may have. I consider it my Sabbath time. It may be only a few minutes squeezed in here or there, but it does bring peace. I may even do a few minor chores like tying a straggling vine to the trellis, deadheading some pansies, or giving a drooping plant a drink. But I approach the garden with no frustration of accomplishing all that needs to be done. I simply accept it for what it is at that moment and love it.

This is much the way God loves us. I'm sure God has special dreams for us, because God created each of us with potential for certain accomplishments. Jesus spoke about the kingdom of heaven, a kingdom that is even now being lived out here on earth. Jesus said, "God's kingdom isn't something you can see. There is no use saying, 'Look! Here it is' or 'Look! There it is.' God's kingdom is here with you" (Luke 17:20-21). We are involved in that kingdom by living to our fullest potential and fulfilling the purposes that God created us for.

Yet we were not made as puppets. God gave each of us an individual will, and sometimes we choose differently. Even so, God continues to love and accept us. As I tell children, God may love us with a happy heart or with a sad heart, but either way, God continues to love us.

I go to my garden for peace, sometimes with a happy heart and sometimes with a sad heart. But I can always find the peace of Sabbath when I let go of my expectations and frustrations, and love my garden for what it is at that moment.

Reflect

~ When have your plans for accomplishment for your garden or another task only ended in frustration?

~ How can you let go of the ambitious plans for your garden and simply enjoy it?

~ What about your garden brings you the most peace?

Pray

God of the garden, I come to you for peace. Thank you for accepting me as a work in progress and loving me just as I am. Amen.

– 31 –

Hammock in My Wooded Garden

God is the one who makes us patient and cheerful. I pray that [God] will help you live at peace with each other, as you follow Christ.

—Romans 15:5

Oh, the joy of a Sabbath time, even on a Thursday in the midst of my writing! It refreshes the soul and clears the mind.

I walked down the steps, past the daylilies that designate the end of our planned garden, past the grassy hill, and stepped into the shade of our wooded garden. Here in the woods, life progresses according to nature's plan. I walked across the carpet of last year's leaves, being careful not to step on the yellow and purple violets that I so admire. I found a new bloom that was not there yesterday, a tiny white bell-like flower, barely raising its head above the leaves.

As I settled myself in the hammock that swings between two medium oaks, the sun filtered through the tall trees overhead. My ears picked out the call of a cardinal among the blended songs of the dozens of wrens and goldfinches that frequent our feeders. Now I rested in the palm of the hammock, simply enjoying the view and loving my Creator. This was a true Sabbath time.

Suddenly, I realized that the pleasant birdcalls had changed to calls of alarm. The bluebird house in our neighbor's woods was the center of the commotion. Birds were dive-bombing the birdhouse from all directions. A downy woodpecker marched anxiously down the side of the tree and back up again. I puzzled over what could cause such upheaval.

I left the peace of the hammock and moved closer to the birdhouse. Then I realized that there was a snake with its head inside the hole of the birdhouse. All of the birds—finches, wrens, and bluebirds—were trying to protect the baby birds inside. Each day I watched these same birds chase one another away from the feeders, but in this time of trouble they bonded together against the predator. They were united in their effort!

I joined the alarm, and my husband and neighbors rushed outside. The snake would not be frightened from the house, and so my husband grabbed its tail and threw it on the ground. Now the birds were safe—at least this time. Although we realize that snakes' preying on eggs or small birds is a natural part of our ecology, our instinct is to assist the defenseless. The surprising thing was how the birds, who otherwise fought one another, were united in their attack against the snake.

Christ was the uniting factor in the lives of Jews and Gentiles in the early church. Christ included those who were outcast during his lifetime. He ate with the detested tax collectors and even talked with women about religion, which was considered a no-no in his day. He told parables about acceptance and sent his disciples to all parts of the world to spread the gospel of God's love.

In one way my Sabbath time was interrupted by the attack of the snake, but in another way it only continued.

Sabbath is about growing closer to God, and the experience certainly helped me do that. I learned from the birds that I can be united with others, even when I don't agree with them about everything. I just hope it doesn't take a violent act to create such unity!

Reflect

~ In what ways do you sometimes unconsciously push others away from their source of soul nourishment?

~ What can you do to make yourself more conscious of those who are left out?

~ How can you bring about unity in ordinary times in the life of your church?

Pray

Help me learn to live in harmony with others, God. I will try to follow Christ's example of inclusiveness. Amen.

– 32 –

Healthy Roots

If the roots of the tree are holy, the rest of the tree is holy too.

—Romans 11:16*b*

At the end of the growing season last year, I was doubtful about the survival of one of my rosebushes. It just didn't look healthy. As spring wore on, I watched the other roses leaf out, but this one just sat there looking dead. Finally, I made the decision that it was beyond help. Even the main stem was black. It was definitely dead. Time to find a replacement.

After a trip to the garden store, I began to dig up the dead rose. To my surprise, there were very few roots, and so the digging was easy. When I pulled it out of the ground, I discovered why. At the base of the rose I discovered a big white worm that had eaten its way into the center of the main stem. The worm was healthy and content in its environment, but it had cut off the source of nourishment for my rose.

Needless to say, I destroyed the worm and treated the ground where I would plant the new rose. But as I threw the dead rosebush in the trash bag, I was reminded of Paul's statement in Romans, and I began to reflect on what keeps the roots of my soul healthy.

It is so easy to let the rush of our schedules press on us and keep us from taking in enough daily nutrients. It's easy to say, "I will be using the Bible as I prepare for this or that lesson, so I will read the Bible then." Or we say, "There will be a devotion time at the meeting I'm attending today, so I'll save time by skipping my meditation time." But those are not the same as personal time spent with God. It's like saying, "I'll be sitting in a meeting with my spouse this afternoon, so I'll not take time for a morning kiss before I leave home." God desires our personal companionship, and we need it to grow—indeed to keep our souls alive.

There is no substitute for that one-on-one time with God. Although Bible study preparation or a devotional heard at a meeting can be occasions where we encounter and experience God, we also need to set aside time to focus solely on God without any other agendas. I must seek that personal relationship. I must remember that time is needed to build that relationship—even to keep it strong. Like the worm in the root of my rose, the hectic pace of my schedule can eat its way into my soul. Allowing the pressure of deadlines and schedules to rob me of my time with God not only cuts off my soul's true source, it also simply adds to my level of stress and frustration.

Our time with God can energize us. When we ignore time with God, we are not nearly as fruitful. We bring about frustration, which in turn creates more stress.

Relationships with other Christians are important for the growth of my soul. God created us to live in community, and those with whom we associate make a difference in our own lives. It's too easy, as an adult, to feel that our personality is formed. Even as adults we are always changing, and the people around us can make a difference in that change.

My soul will grow through study—both study of the scriptures and study of the writings of people today to whom, and through whom, God has spoken. God did not stop inspiring people with the canonization of the Bible. God continues to speak, and the messages of today's prophets can bring about soul growth.

Reflection is one of the best ways to help my soul grow. I reflect best with a pen in my hand or my fingers on a computer keyboard. Some people reflect best by listening to music, and some of us need quiet. For me, it is through quiet that I find the opportunity to have that one-on-one time with God. I may not form any words in my mind, but in that quiet I know that God and I are together. I know that God is nourishing my soul.

Only through the roots could the rose receive nourishment, and only if we keep our soul roots healthy can we expect it to grow.

Reflect

~ What keeps your soul roots healthy?

~ What have you done on days when you've felt God with you every step of the way? What have you not done on days when you've felt cut off from God?

~ What specific change can you make in your life today to help your soul grow?

Pray

Too often I rush through life, Lord. Remind me that I must stop to grow my soul. Remind me of your presence and urge me to stop and live in that presence. Amen.

– 33 –

Short Sabbaths

Right away, Jesus made his disciples get into the boat and start back across to Bethsaida. But he stayed until he had sent the crowds away. Then he told them good-by and went up on the side of a mountain to pray.

—Mark 6:45-46

There comes a time in each day when we must get away. Sometimes we can only get away in our minds, but even those short Sabbaths can make a difference in how our days turn out.

In the midst of my writing, I often leave my desk for a short trip to the kitchen window or the back screened-in porch. It is the pause that refreshes. I stand with my arms on the top of the lower window or sit briefly on the porch, gazing into my garden and the woods beyond. I use my eyes to refresh my spirits. Visually I go beyond the small ferns I planted in the opening to the woods. I journey with my eyes past the large pines and the low dogwoods—back, back, back between the new oaks and poplars, even past the slender hickory, until I can't distinguish one tree from another. There is only a blanket of green with brown bark peeking through at places. My eyes seem to search beyond all that I see, entering the soul of the forest.

Is this the concept of eternity? Is this the way it feels to see forever? Though we will never have complete understanding of eternity in this life, for me this seems to be as close as it comes: to look into the depths of the forest and never see the end.

My mother's Sabbath experience of eternity was quite different from mine. The forest and trees made her feel hemmed in. I grew up roaming the live oak forests of central Florida, but she grew up on the plains of New Mexico where there were few trees in sight. It filled her soul to be able to look into the distance without anything blocking her vision. Experiencing eternity for her would have been reaching into the soul of the horizon, searching but never finding the place where the earth meets the sky.

It is important to take Sabbaths, no matter how we take time for them. They refresh our body and spirit, and they feed the soul. I find mine in the garden and beyond; my mother found hers in the horizon. Sabbaths fill our souls like the cup of a desert well, full and running over.

Reflect

~ Where can you find strength by searching for eternity?

~ What fills your soul in the midst of a rushed day?

~ How can you make use of short Sabbaths during the day?

Pray

Lord, give me insight into eternity. Grant me short Sabbath opportunities, and I will try to take advantage of them. Amen.

My Garden Smooths Out Rough Edges

– 34 –

On Rainy Days and Hummingbirds

Faith that doesn't lead us to do good deeds is all alone and dead!
—James 2:17

It was a very rainy day—one of those days when you think the sun has forgotten how to shine. It had rained for several days, and everything was sodden with moisture. I had not seen a bird at our garden feeders for some time, and I wondered how the little creatures could survive without food.

Suddenly a streak of color flew past my window, and a small hummingbird landed on the feeder perch. As the rain fell around her, the hummer sucked up the nourishing sugar water. Periodically she fluttered her wings, shaking off the accumulation of rainwater. Presently, she gave her wings a final flutter and flew away.

It occurred to me that we are much like this rainy weather hummingbird. We must seek out the source of our spiritual nourishment, even in dreary times. The opportunities may not come to us, but we can find them even in the dimly lit days of our lives. This sometimes means venturing forth into some unpleasant weather, and it sometimes means facing cloudy skies.

When we do find our spiritual source, we are tempted to spend all of our time soaking in that nourishment, ignoring the conditions of the world around us. We become very self-centered. When we finally wake up to the world around us and try to fly, we may find that our wings have become waterlogged with the damp dreariness of the world; and we wish to remain sluggishly sitting on the roost of our complacent religious perches. To fly to greater heights spiritually, we must periodically flutter our wings, keeping them ready by putting our energy into action. Without such spiritual "muscle-building" action, we will never negotiate the opportunities to fly to greater heights on our divine journeys.

Reflect

~ What dreary days have you experienced in your spiritual life?

~ What Christian action opportunities have you missed when you have been too self-centered in you own spiritual search?

~ How can you become more alert to these opportunities?

Pray

God of the hummingbird, make me alert to the sluggishness of my spiritual life. Give me the wisdom to keep my wings active in service to others so that I may mount up on dry wings, flying to heights unknown to me before. Amen.

– 35 –

A Gardener's Point of View

Honor God by accepting each other, as Christ has accepted you.

—Romans 15:7

Surveying the rows of new bedding plants at the local garden store, I came upon a familiar flower. It was a flower I remembered, but I had never seen it in a garden store or expected to see it there. It was a weed I remembered from my childhood, sporting itself as a legitimate flower to be purchased and cultivated.

Lantana was never cultivated in the gardens of my childhood. It was simply a roadside flower, enduring the wheels of cars and extreme drought conditions. The flower would show itself now and then in gardens, but not for long! Any gardener worth his or her salt would have dug it up and thrown it out. But now, in recent years, we have come to accept this reject of the past. Now we are seeing the plant through the eyes of God who made it.

I purchased the lantana and watched it grow, spreading its runners just as God intended it to do. Each time I saw the flower head with its nest of petals, I thought about the many people we reject because we are told that they are not appropriate for our garden of friends: people of a different color or culture; people who make less or more money than we; people who have religious beliefs different from ours. In fact, sometimes in a religious community we become so elite and self-centered that we can see only ourselves and those who believe as we do.

Yet God made each person in God's own image, just as God made the lantana and the rose. God gave us all the capability of finding God in our own way. You may not understand or worship God the same way, but your way is also legitimate.

If every person is important to God, then why not also to me? Sometimes we don't recognize our attitude of rejection. We simply ignore the person or go our merry way, pretending that he or she isn't there. We live with the attitude, "Ignore it and it will go away." But God made us to be in relationship with one another, as well as in relationship with God. Just as the lantana emerged as a legitimate flower after surviving beside the road and being ignored for years, we can recognize those whom the world rejects as unique and beloved children of God by seeing them through God's eyes.

Reflect

~ Whom do you reject simply by ignoring them?

~ What positive aspects of your life are sometimes ignored by others? How does this make you feel?

~ How can you put yourself in the shoes of someone who is rejected? What can you do to make him or her feel accepted and loved?

Pray

God of the rejected, help me accept each person, just as Christ has accepted me in spite of my unloving ways. Amen.

– 36 –

The Way Made Easy

"I am the way, the truth, and the life!" Jesus answered. "Without me, no one can go to the Father."

—John 14:6

For almost two years, we climbed down and up the forty-five-degree drop-off behind our house to get into the woods. There was a small clearing that we began to develop into a wooded garden, but dragging equipment and hoses up and down the hill became a chore. The developer had put large rocks in the gulley that drained the water off our lawn. We used these rocks to climb back up to the house rather than slipping on the grass of the incline. Some of the rocks finally settled into the ground with the flat sides up, giving us a more solid stepping surface. But the rocks were treacherous, and every step of the way I expected to twist an ankle.

Recently my husband finished a series of steps leading down the hill. Now we have an easier way, a guided path. This reminded me of Jesus' statement to his disciples that he had come to give us an easier way.

Jesus' claim can be taken in two ways. The second part of this verse—"Without me, no one can go to the Father"—has sometimes caused churches to become exclusive. They see themselves as select, as the only way of salvation. But Jesus claimed to be the way, and if we look at his life it was not one of elitism. Jesus' way was inclusive. Jesus reached out to every person, whether that person agreed with him or not. In fact, in Mark 7:24-30 we read how Jesus reconsidered his ministry and included the woman from Syria. She came to Jesus, searching for healing for her daughter. Jesus did not ask her if she believed in the same theological principles as he. He did not say, "Will you bow down and worship me?" In fact, she was forward enough to dispute his theory of helping the Jewish community first, and he reconsidered. Jesus did not block her path.

If Jesus is the way, then we must pattern our lives after his. We're only giving lip service to Jesus if we only mouth the words. Jesus taught and modeled action. Again and again, he told people to give to the poor, care for the underprivileged, and see that the ill have healing. When he was a dinner guest of an important Pharisee, Jesus told his host that he should also invite the poor, the crippled, the lame, and the blind to his banquets. Family and rich neighbors could return the favor by inviting him to their houses for a meal, but the poor and afflicted folks were not able to do so. Giving without any expectation of return is the true way to be hospitable.

Following Jesus' way means giving of oneself unselfishly to serve and care for others. This way is the sure path of steps as opposed to the treacherous rocks.

Reflect

~ How do you understand Jesus' way? How do you follow it?

~ What can you do in your own environment to be open to and inclusive of everyone?

~ Who does not agree with you theologically whom you can reach out to in love—not trying to change his or her beliefs, but simply in love?

Pray

I am thankful, Lord, for the way that Jesus taught and modeled. Give me the courage to break out of my comfortable shell and reach out to others who are different from me or who believe differently. Amen.

– 37 –

Rebirth from Fire

Dear friends, don't be surprised or shocked that you are going through testing that is like walking through fire. Be glad for the chance to suffer as Christ suffered. It will prepare you for even greater happiness when he makes his glorious return. Count it a blessing when you suffer for being a Christian. This shows that God's glorious Spirit is with you. If you suffer for obeying God, you must have complete faith in your faithful Creator and keep on doing right.

—1 Peter 4:12-14, 19

Pine straw is the favorite mulch for gardens in my area of the country. Each year we replenish the beds, spreading the brown needles around the house and trees. Part of the package, however, is that a small crop of seedling pines also sprouts. This is no problem, as long as we pull them during their first summer.

The seeds from these pines naturally fall out of the open cones. There are pinecones, however, that do not open and release their seeds until they are exposed to excessive heat. God has provided for the replenishing of the earth, even after intense heat has killed every other vegetation in a forest.

Just as the seeds of these cones are protected, and just as the heat of the blaze brings about the correct circumstances for the seeds to reproduce, we can know that God protects us with love. God protects us even through the fiery trials in our lives. These times can often produce more spiritual growth than the calm, cooling spiritual encounters.

Leslie Weatherhead, a pastor in England during World War II, preached several sermons to help his parishioners deal with the flaming trials they were encountering. These sermons became a classic book that has helped many deal with God's will. Weatherhead suggested that when we talk about the "will of God" we really mean several different things. He therefore distinguished God's will into three categories:

> ~ the intentional or original will—God's original intention was that we should live in loving relationship with God and with one another. However, we were also given the ability to make our own choices.

> ~ the circumstantial will—Because we have been allowed by God to make our choices, we create circumstances that may not be in God's original intention. This is God's circumstantial will because God allows it.

> ~ the ultimate will—When we work with God, the circumstances of our choices (even if they are not good) are used to restore our relationship with God. Ultimately God's will prevails.

To fulfill the ultimate will of God, we must release our trials so that the growth may come about. God can use those experiences to refine us if we release them and let it happen. We are forever changed, just like the seed is forever changed. Those seeds of God's love can take root in the ashes of the fires of our lives and enable God to grow our souls.

Reflect

~ What trials have you seen in your life?

~ How has God used those problems to help you grow spiritually?

~ What is troubling you in your life right now? How can you turn it over to God in order to help your soul grow?

Pray

I thank you, God, for the trials in my life, although I know that you did not put them there purposely. Help me use those times to grow my soul. Amen.

– 38 –

The Unexpected

At noon the sky turned dark and stayed that way until three o'clock. Then about that time Jesus shouted, "Eli, Eli, lema sabachthani?" which means, "My God, my God, why have you deserted me?"

—Matthew 27:45-46

I was anxious to plant some color around the base of our new home. We stopped at a new discount center with its expanded garden store to check out the plants. Among the perennials I found the plants I thought would do the trick. As I gazed at the picture on the plant tab, I envisioned the bright red flowers emerging on their stalks over a low blanket of greenery. I planted them just under our bedroom window. All summer long they remained green, but never put out the red flowers. Where were the blazing red blooms that were pictured? Where was the excitement?

Perhaps this is how we sometimes feel about our "God experiences." They don't turn out as we expected them. We hear of people who have a dramatic conversion experience, and we wonder what is wrong with us because we've not had such an encounter with God. We must realize that God comes to each of us in different ways. The Bible gives us many examples of ways that people have experienced God. Abraham had many one-on-one encounters with God, and God also came to him through other men. Moses experienced God through a burning bush and on a mountaintop. Elijah did not find God in a strong wind, an earthquake, or fire; rather, God came to him in a gentle breeze. Paul was struck down and stopped dead in his tracks when he experienced God. Yet Paul also affirmed the gradual experience of God that Timothy had through the training of his mother and grandmother.

Or we may recall times when we have had a deeply emotional experience with God, but now it seems that nothing moves us. We often speak of these as the dry times in our spiritual lives. Jesus experienced such a time on the cross when he cried out "My God, my God, why have you forsaken me?" (Matthew 27:46 NRSV). Those times are not necessarily dry. We can be assured that God is with us at all times in many unique ways, though we may be unaware of God's presence. We expect one revelation of God; yet God comes to us in different and surprising ways.

Rather than expecting to find God in the same manner that others have, we must be alert to God's presence in all of life. Acknowledging those "Wow, there's God!" moments brings appreciation.

As the summer came to an end, I realized that my bedroom window plants were not going to bloom, at least not that year. Instead, I appreciated the lush carpet of green that they provided. It was a different experience. There were no flashing streaks of red blowing in the wind. Nothing grew high above the windowsill. But nonetheless, as I looked out my window, the carpet of green was pleasing to the eyes. I was glad that I had bought the plants, and I will continue to tend them with care.

Reflect

~ When have you had startling spiritual encounters with God? When have you also grown quietly in God's love?

~ When have you felt that you were spiritually drawing from a "dry well," only to find God's revelation in a different way?

~ Who has been an agent of God for you, as Abram's visitors were agents of God? (Genesis 18)

Pray

My God, you show yourself to me in many different ways. Help me recognize you and draw closer to you throughout each day. Amen.

– 39 –

The Time of Singing

Winter is past, the rain has stopped; flowers cover the earth, it's time to sing. The cooing of doves is heard in our land.

—Song of Solomon 2:11-12

Springtime had come in my garden. I was enjoying an early opportunity to connect with the earth. Above me a variety of birds were singing their hearts out. My thoughts turned to the biblical poem attributed to King Solomon. I knew that the birds I heard weren't turtledoves, but as far as I was concerned, they were as lovely as any turtledove.

Suddenly the birds hushed their singing, and almost as quickly, I heard the raucous sound of a huge flock of grackles. They swooped in like a black cloud and settled on the limbs of nearby trees, cackling their pleasure. I lifted my rake and shook it at them. I even gave them a piece of my mind for breaking up the lovely voices of my birds! How could I have a peaceful time with God in the midst of those shrieking birds?

Then God gave me a thought. Do the grackles have any other voice with which to praise God? Who gave them a voice in the first place? We were each given a voice according to God's desire. Who was I to scold these large black birds for using the only voice that they had?

How many times do we react in the same way? We complain about contemporary music in church, or that the songs are slow and lifeless. We complain that the service is too formal and stuffy, or that there is no liturgy. We complain that the worship area is like every other worship area in town, or we complain that the worship area has no symbolic significance. We complain that our worship services are not welcoming, or we complain that the greeting time breaks into our worship experience.

Each person must seek God in his or her own way. We have no right to demand that everyone worship in the same manner as we. God made us unique in our personalities, and that personality makes a difference in how we best seek God. Who am I to demand that worship be planned in only one way? Who am I to complain that God set different desires in each of us?

I put down my rake and began to sing, "Morning has broken like the first morning; blackbird has spoken like the first bird. Praise for the singing! Praise for the morning! Praise for them, springing fresh from the Word."

Reflect

~ When have you complained because worship was not conducted as you thought it should be?

~ Do you know someone who worships differently? Does this affect your relationship with this person?

~ How can you give others permission to praise God in the manner that best suits them?

Pray

God of the grackles, give me the wisdom to recognize the many different ways that people worship you. Amen.

My Garden Recycles Life

– 40 –

Nurtured Over Tough Times

Apollos and I are merely servants who helped you to have faith. It was the Lord who made it all happen. I planted the seeds, Apollos watered them, but God made them sprout and grow.

—1 Corinthians 3:5-6

We moved into a new house with planting beds established around the foundation. These beds were covered with pine straw, common mulch for that area of the country. It was fall, but the cold weather had held off long enough for some weeds to sprout in the beds. I anticipated planting azaleas in the spring, but before winter really set in, I decided to pull the few weeds emerging. As I turned the corner of the house, there near the downspout was a plant that I recognized. Now how, I wondered, could a tomato plant be growing in this fresh soil dredged up and tossed around by a backhoe?

The source would remain a mystery, but I could not bring myself to simply discard this gift of a tomato plant. If I left it in the ground it would surely die with the first frost. So I found a pot and brought the seedling indoors.

All winter long it sat on a shelf in front of our bedroom window, putting forth little growth but holding its own among my philodendron and ivy. There were times when I wasn't sure this orphan plant would make it to spring, but I continued to water it with an occasional jolt of fertilizer.

Finally, the danger of frost was past, and I carefully moved the tomato back outside where God's nurturing elements could take over. Between the sun and the washing rains, the plant grew taller and taller. Soon, my tomato cage could not contain it. It grew above the top wires and spilled over the sides.

I delighted in the first blooms! At times I've had to spray a special formula on tomatoes to bring on the fruit, but not with this plant! Tiny fruits appeared as soon as the blossoms wilted, and I imagined the large red spheres that would soon be lining my kitchen cupboard. Then to my surprise, the tomatoes grew in an elongated form. I had Roma tomatoes, the specialty tomatoes of Italian cooks! I have never eaten more delicious tomatoes, and the plant produced all summer, gifting us with its sweetness.

I had nurtured the plant over some tough times—times when all the elements it needed for real growth were not available. But when the time came and the right circumstances were there, growth could not be denied!

How like life that is. We have tough times when growth seems impossible, and we may become discouraged in the winters of life. Then someone comes along and nurtures us over those rough times, just barely keeping us on course. Finally, we find ourselves in God's sunshine, with the rain washing from above, and our roots reach out for more nourishment. We expand our horizons and begin to bear fruit!

Reflect

~ When have you had someone help you over tough times? Have you thanked him or her for it lately?

~ Whom do you know today who is experiencing a "winter" of life?

~ What can you do to help that person make it to spring?

Pray

God, give me appreciation for those who have nurtured me, and help me seek out the opportunities to help others in their bleak moments. Amen.

– 41 –

Where's the Love Grass?

A farmer went out to scatter seed in a field. While the farmer was scattering the seed, some of it fell along the road and was eaten by birds. Other seeds fell on thin, rocky ground and quickly started growing because the soil wasn't very deep. But when the sun came up, the plants were scorched and dried up, because they did not have enough roots. Some other seeds fell where thornbushes grew up and choked out the plants. . . . But a few seeds did fall on good ground where the plants grew and produced thirty or sixty or even a hundred times as much as was scattered.

—Mark 4:3-9

We stood with the representative from our developer. We had been in our new home for eleven months. Before us was the forty-five-degree slope behind our house that leads down to a wooded area. On that slope were a dozen sprigs of love grass and a multitude of weeds. We had been promised love grass when we wrote the contract on the house.

Love grass is a favorite grass for banks along the highways. It is supposed to be maintenance free. It grows about one and a half to two feet tall and then lies over, creating a cascading blanket of grass that does not need cutting. Now the truth lay before us—we had weeds, not love grass.

Planting this grass in the spring or early summer gives it strong roots before the frost. But ours was planted in the fall, along with rye to give it protection as it sprouted. The rye was supposed to die out and the love grass flourish. Instead, the love grass seedlings died, and the miscellaneous seeds from the straw cover took over. Our developer promised to kill the weeds in the spring and replant the love grass.

This experience reminded me of Jesus' parable. Sometimes we don't prepare the ground for our spiritual growth, and sometimes we push our spirituality, expecting growth in the wrong situations. The climate and setting for each person's spirituality is different, and what is right for me may not be right for you. I may need more quiet time. You may need a high-energy worship. Someone else may grow spiritually primarily through service to others. We must all find our own paths to growing our souls.

Reflect

~ When has your spiritual quest seemed to take root and flourish? What environmental factors helped?

~ When has your spiritual quest seemed to die? What was happening then?

~ How can you increase your commitment to spiritual growth?

Pray

God of the weeds and grasses, I know that you love me even when my spiritual growth seems to stand still. I turn to a new season now, and I will look for the right opportunities to grow closer to you. Amen.

– 42 –

Life-giving Water

Have faith in me, and you will have life-giving water flowing from deep inside you, just as the Scriptures say.

—John 7:38

Some years ago we decided to build a pond in our garden. Over the years our pond became a joy for us and a life-giving part of the lives of several animals that frequented our yard. Water is a soothing part of any garden, whether it is in a pond or a small lake, or even a recycling fountain.

We can learn about life from water—no matter whether it is pure and deep, broad and salty, constantly flowing, or even stagnant.

Everything that God created has a purpose. God created the swamps as well as the sparkling clear streams. Sometimes in our ignorance we try to eliminate swamps. Most of the south central part of Florida is what we have named the Everglades. This used to be considered a swamp, but now we recognize that it is actually a widespread, slowly flowing river. This area of Florida is almost impossible to cross without roads. Years ago there was an attempt to change the structure of the area and drain the water, causing more damage than good. Now we realize that this movement of water is necessary. This swamp is being used.

In my garden I sometimes have stagnant water filling the low places after a heavy rain. The ground may be so saturated that it is unable to absorb an additional ounce. Then the water breeds mosquitoes and can develop a stale odor. Where the water flows off, this doesn't happen.

It is important for us to receive the blessings that contribute to our spiritual growth. With those opportunities we grow and mature as God wants us to. But if we simply absorb blessings and seek only to fill our own needs, then we can become stagnant. We ask ourselves why life has become mundane, even as we are trying to fill it with God. We must allow God's blessings to flow through us, purifying us as we pass the blessings on to others. We must be in service to others as well as in search of opportunities to grow ourselves.

The water on this earth is never depleted, only recycled in some way. But if it sits stagnant without movement, the recycling process is blocked. Likewise, God's blessings are all around us, but if we don't pass them on to others, we soon become complacent about our blessings, and our spiritual growth is blocked.

Reflect

~ Have you become self-centered as you search for opportunities to increase your own spirituality?

~ What blessings do you find that you can share with others?

~ To whom can you be a channel for God's blessings?

Pray

Thank you for the many blessings, Lord. Help me be like a flowing stream, channeling your love to others. Amen.

– 43 –

Recycled Beliefs

But the LORD created the stars and put them in place. [God] turns darkness to dawn and daylight to darkness; [God] scoops up the ocean and empties it on the earth.

—Amos 5:8

The rain fell steadily on the garden, softening the hard-packed dirt. It had been weeks since we had had any measurable rain, and now I looked out the window at the life-giving moisture with gratitude.

As I watched the sheets of rain run down my windowpane, I recalled how I believed rain was made as a child. About once a year our family drove from Florida to the northern panhandle of Texas to visit my grandmother. I remembered the year that Texas had been experiencing a severe drought. The creek beds had dried up, leaving a crazed pattern of dried mud. All around me, I heard adults praying for rain. The only way I could understand the pleading prayers of the adults was to believe that they were trying to convince God to make it rain. In my concrete mind God was a superhuman being living above us in the clouds. I imagined God taking an ice pick and poking holes in the clouds. Then, this super-human God of my imagination would take a dipper—similar to the dipper at my grandmother's pump—and pour water over the clouds, providing rain for the praying world.

Obviously, I no longer hold that image of God. I recognize that God has planned a way to recycle water, drawing it up from the earth and returning it to earth as rain. Just how that is done I leave to God and to the scientists to comprehend.

Just as I have recycled my scientific knowledge, I have also recycled my belief in prayer. I no longer see prayer as a way of hounding God to obey our biddings, but rather a way to lay our problems before the most loving and caring God we can know. Through sharing our problems, we grow closer to this personal God. The rain may not fall when we would like, or the rain may fall on our parade. In either case, prayer helps us continue to develop a relationship that can weather everything that comes our way in life.

As I question and inquire into my various beliefs, I grow spiritually. My faith deepens with each query, and although my beliefs may change, my faith remains steadfast.

Reflect

~ What beliefs of the past have you worked through and recycled?

~ What beliefs have you worked through and still found to be true today?

~ How can you be a clarifier for others, encouraging them to feel free to inquire into their beliefs and thereby grow in their faith?

Pray

God of thinking, give me the earnestness to search through my beliefs. Help me realize that unless I truly search, my beliefs will never be my own, only those of someone else that I have tagged as mine. Amen.

– 44 –

Apple Trees and Twin Girls

Come, my children, listen as I teach you to respect the LORD.
—Psalm 34:11

Last year we planted two apple trees that were different though their leaves looked identical. This year we are caring for our new twin granddaughters each day. Most people cannot tell them apart. Yet each is a unique individual with a mind and spirit of her own.

We were instructed to dig a hole twice the size of the root ball when planting our apple trees. Trees need lots of room to spread their roots. Those of us who care for children must create large holes in our lives. Everything changes. Our house now looks like a nursery with two of almost everything. We've created a big hole in our lives, not only physically, but also emotionally and spiritually. And what a joy to watch them fill it with their smiles and hugs!

Our apple trees need tending. We must protect them from hazardous insects and supply them with any lacking nutrients. In the dry season, we must water them frequently. Children must be protected when they are young and taught to protect themselves as they leave our care. Children not only need physical nutrients to grow, but their souls also need love and caring. The love that adults show to children is the first Bible that a child will "read."

Loving a child lays the foundation for faith and for a true understanding of God's love.

We first bought only one apple tree, but later purchased another when we read that our tree would need another to reproduce. Children thrive best in community, especially in Christian community. Not only do parents and care-givers need to create holes for children, but our church families must also. Each Sunday we sit in worship with the twins amid other caring adults. The girls are often passed from one loving embrace to another. Each new child is welcomed with a rose on the altar and into the loving arms of the congregation. This is the true hospitality of Christ.

Our apple trees will be different from other apple trees. They will all produce apples, but their shape and structure will be different, depending on how they are tended and pruned. Life prunes our children, and we parents and caregivers tend them. They may not turn out exactly as we imagined, but they are all images of God and should be loved no matter what their shape.

Reflect

~ What children do you know who reflect God?

~ What children do you find hard to love? How can you remind yourself that they are made in the image of God?

~ How can your church be more welcoming to children?

Pray

God of us all, help me remember the opportunities to show your love to children. Measure the holes in my life and make them large enough to include those children around me. Amen.

– 45 –

Thirsty Plants

You are my God. I worship you. In my heart, I long for you, as I would long for a stream in a scorching desert.

—Psalm 63:1

I have a plant that I cherish called Joseph's coat. It is a simple plant with only a tiny blossom, but it has a splash of maroon, yellow, and green in its leaves. I cherish it not for its blooms or color but because a dear friend who died of cancer gave it to me. I don't even remember the occasion, but she picked a rose from her garden, placed a couple of sprigs of Joseph's coat in the vase, and brought it to me. She assured me that it would root in water and could then be planted.

I kept a pot of the tiny plant flourishing for two years, and then moved the plant outdoors where it grew for six years. Each winter I would bring in a few slips and root them, just in case the Florida winters got too cold. When we moved from Florida to north Georgia, sprigs from the plant came along. Last summer I again put the plant in the garden. However, it was not at an obvious place, and during a drought I failed to water it. By the time I caught my mistake, the plant was limp, and many of the leaves had dried up. Once watered, the plant perked up. But when I rooted sprigs this winter, I again failed to water it. Although it did not die, the plant struggled all winter.

No life on earth is possible without water. You can live

for more than a month without food, but less than a week without water. Water is not only life-giving, it is also life-refreshing. Water is necessary for drinking, for cleanliness, for refreshment, and even for producing our other daily needs.

Our souls are much like my plant and its need for water. A soul is lifeless without God. As the psalmist said, our souls long for God much as we would long for fresh, flowing water in the midst of a desert. If we don't replenish our spiritual water source, our souls will wither and die. It is our responsibility to seek out the source of our enrichment and take advantage of it. God placed a thirst within us that only God can fill. We may try filling it with all the popular trappings of this world, but only the thirst-quenching presence of God will fill that thirst.

Reflect

~ What have you been trying to use to quench your spiritual thirst?

~ Where can you find true life-giving water for your soul?

~ How can you share that life-giving water with others?

Pray

God, I come before you as a child comes to the mother with specific needs. Give me the evidence of your nurturing water. Amen.

My Garden Opportunities, Lost and Found

– 46 –

Seeds and Change

Let the Spirit change your way of thinking and make you into a new person. You were created to be like God, and so you must please [God] and be truly holy.

—Ephesians 4:23-24

The variety of seeds never ceases to amaze me. How could God create so many varieties of seeds? Some seeds are so minute that you can hardly see them. I recently planted lettuce seeds, and they looked like small broken pieces of grass. Some seeds are large and wrinkled, like beet seeds. Some seeds stick to clothing, and some have wings and drift in the wind like helicopters or cotton fluff.

No matter what the seed looks like, it changes and becomes the plant that was intended. There are certain outside influences that cause the seed to change, such as moisture and temperature. In order for the plant to grow there must be nourishment.

I sometimes wonder if I am not like a sprouting seed, constantly changing and becoming a new person. But at other times I resist change. Does that stunt my growth?

Does a seed bemoan the fact that it is changing—that outside forces are intruding on it, softening it and "spoiling" it? Imagine a seed saying, "Life isn't what it used to be!" How absurd for a seed to think thus. But sometimes I fail to accept what comes to me, and I fail to look for the good opportunities for growth that it may yield. The spreading fruit tree doesn't curse the rain that caused it to sprout—it opens its arms to more rain, recognizing the value of change each day.

From the beginning of time, we have learned to bring positive results from change. Abraham accepted change and moved his family. Out of that came a new nation. Joseph accepted change and adjusted to living in Egypt, far from his family. He was later able to save his family when drought came. New worlds have been explored, and nations established because of change.

Change can bring about new ideas too. If the Hebrews had lived an idyllic life in Egypt, they would never have had to struggle with their concepts of God, and we might well believe in a God who has no concern for people.

A seed cannot refuse to grow when the God-given powers of sun and rain are in its atmosphere. It *must* burst out of its casing. We are that way when God takes over our lives. We cannot remain comfortable in our shells, refusing change. The seed must burst open, and it continues to change as it matures. Likewise, we must burst open and die to the old life in order to be born anew. And unless we continue to change, we become stunted in our spiritual development and cannot yield fruit.

Reflect

~ How is your soul like a seed? What agent does God use to soften the outer shell?

~ When have you resisted change only to find that it made a new beginning for you?

~ Are there multiple opportunities to break out of old casings and grow? What opportunities do you face today?

Pray

Use your softening agents, God, and prepare me for change. Help me look at these opportunities as moments of growth and not let them slip by me. Amen.

– 47 –

Different Oaks for Different Folks

Welcome all the Lord's followers, even those whose faith is weak. Don't criticize them for having beliefs that are different from yours.

—Romans 14:1

Behind our house is a wooded area that drains into a Corps of Engineers lake. It will always be protected, and it is covered with a variety of trees that have grown since the last logging, probably fifty to seventy-five years ago. There are no three- and four-hundred-year-old trees, as some areas can boast, but the trees are still stately and proud.

To some people, the trees are just trees. But I find joy in noticing the differences in the trees and identifying them. Indeed, I can spend hours plowing through a tree book trying to find the exact identification of a tree. The color and texture of the trunk, the size and shape of the leaves and acorns, even the general shape of the tree are all characteristics to consider when identifying a tree. My tree book lists thirty-one different oaks alone. But the interesting thing is that, just as different persons born of the same parents have different DNA, an oak is an oak, even when it has different leaves and acorns, and a palm is a palm, even when the fronds grow in a different manner.

I visited a friend when we lived in Florida who had a lovely queen palm beside his house. I commented on the palm, expressing my appreciation for such a majestic tree.

To my surprise he did not like the tree. He claimed it was messy, dropping its seeds throughout most of the year. He showed me the many palm seedlings that had sprouted around the base of the tree among his shrubs.

Asking his permission, I carefully pulled up a dozen or so seedlings and placed them in a plastic bag to take home. After a couple of years in pots, I had three queen palms ready to plant in my own garden and several to share with neighbors. When we moved from that house, the palms had reached the second story of our home.

In that same Florida city, I discovered a garden of palms. It amazed me that there were so many different varieties, and the garden became one of the regular stops on our tours for out-of-town guests. Friends from out of the state sometimes said that Florida had no variety, only palm trees and sand. Most palms do have only subtle differences. Being alert to those differences can help us realize that everything is created according to God's purpose.

A friend of mine once said, "Variety is the spice of life, and I like mine very spicy!" God could have made the world in black and white, and we'd never have known the difference. God could have made each tree alike, and each flower and blade of grass the same. Think what we would miss if every bird or butterfly was like every other one. And think what a dull life we would live if every person not only looked alike, but also thought in the same manner. There would be no lively conversations, no reason to share ideas, and no opportunity to explore new thoughts and grow our souls.

As I enjoy the large variety of trees in my garden and just beyond, I think of people with whom I've discussed different beliefs. Each conversation brought me to a better understanding of my own beliefs, whether I agreed with them or not. Opening the door to those conversations sometimes comes only with difficulty. We'd rather sit in our own little room with our familiar surroundings instead of stepping to the door and shoving it open to the fresh air of diverse thoughts. But if we close that door, we will miss the opportunities to live in fellowship with those who have different beliefs from ours.

Reflect

~ What beliefs have you adjusted in recent years because of a conversation with a friend or colleague?

~ What beliefs do you have that you are keeping behind closed doors for fear of confronting those with different opinions?

~ What can you use as opening opportunity for discussion, such as a book or film?

Pray

I don't want my soul to become stale, Lord. I need opportunities to look at things from all perspectives. Please send persons who will give me new insights, and help me open my door to them. Amen.

– 48 –

Atmosphere for Growth

I planted the seeds, Apollos watered them, but God made them sprout and grow.

—1 Corinthians 3:6

My rhododendron is not doing well in my garden. This is its second spring, and it continues to drop dry leaves and an occasional limb. What did I do wrong?

Each week our newspaper has a special gardening section that I often cut out and keep. In my search for the article on rhododendrons, I found a possible answer. This lovely mountain bush thrives when it has lots of water, but it doesn't like its roots constantly wet. I must have read that when I planted the bush, because I had made sure that the water didn't settle around the roots. But I think I had made too sure of it! The water drains off the mound where it is planted so rapidly that it doesn't soak in at all. The only time it really gets any water to the roots is when we have constant rain all day. The plant is also quite close to the building, so sometimes it doesn't get much moisture even when it rains.

Now I must find a new place for this plant—one that allows the water to soak in, but doesn't remain soggy. After some thought, I decided to move it to the edge of the woods behind the house. It will not show from the street, but why do I need to put on a flower show for other people anyway?

One of the secrets of gardening is creating an atmosphere of growth for each plant. When I move the rhododendron, I will build a little cup or dam around it to hold the water. My wild Cherokee rose has outgrown its space, so it will also have to be moved. The clematis likes to have its roots shaded, but my roses need a great deal of sunshine. My hostas also need shade. Every plant has its own individual growth needs, and I must respect their needs if I want to have lovely plants.

The same is true with growing our souls. Recent study indicates that our personalities have much to do with the way we grow spiritually. Extroverts find small group encounters and corporate worship helpful, and Introverts appreciate personal meditation and contemplative worship. Those who take in information through their senses (Sensers) enjoy music, touch, smells, and action in their worship, and those who take in information through a mental process (Intuitives) enjoy in-depth study, journaling, and reading thoughts that other people have written. Those who make their decisions based on feelings (Feelers) grow spiritually as they involve themselves in the lives of others, and those who go through a logical process to make decisions (Thinkers) apply their personal lives to study and appreciate liturgy and symbols. Persons who like to organize their lives in a precise manner (Judgers) lay out goals for their specific study/prayer time and create prayer lists, whereas persons who are more spontaneous in their decisions (Perceivers) look for new methods and spontaneous opportunities of prayer.

We must spend as much effort in creating the right atmosphere for our spiritual growth as we do in creating the right garden atmosphere for plants. It is too easy to adopt the attitude that the soul will take care of itself!

Reflect

~ Have you been approaching your spiritual gardening with the right methods for your own personality, or do you need to consider changing?

~ How do you consciously prepare for your spiritual growth?

~ What can you prune from your life in order to have the necessary time?

Pray

You have given me a certain personality, God, with specific spiritual needs. Give me the wisdom and tools to create the environment I need to grow my soul. Amen.

– 49 –

Deadheading

Each of you must make up your own mind about how much to give. But don't feel sorry that you must give and don't feel that you are forced to give. God loves people who love to give.

—2 Corinthians 9:7

The garden books tell me that if I cut blooms from the stems of certain flowers, they will continue to bloom throughout the summer. If I let them go to seed, then their blooming season will be cut short. But it takes time to deadhead these plants. It puts a strain on my time budget! How much easier to simply let them bloom and run their course. If, however, I want to continue to have flowers, I must spend the time.

Deadheading for flowers works much like giving in our spiritual lives. If we give, we will continue to grow and develop more gifts. But if we hoard our time and talents, we will become stagnant and what gifts we have will die. This is true of any talent that God has given us.

My gift of writing lay dormant during my early years. I knew I could accomplish a writing assignment in school, but I had no idea that I could actually write something that people would want to read or that would help others grow closer to God. One year a friend and I worked as aides in our local high school. At her urging, I began taking notes in a notebook as we walked around the resource center, carrying out our job of keeping order among the students. After work each day, we went to a local coffee shop and reviewed our notes—mainly thoughts on life for high school students as well as life in general. She helped me realize that I did have a gift for writing.

My writing could have remained something that I did to clear my mind or something that I used for self-satisfaction. However, God seemed to urge me on to more writing opportunities. I took a correspondence course and began writing some feature articles for magazines and newspapers, as well as a weekly column. The pay was minimal, but I spent hours struggling over the correct words. Some years later when I needed a resource for workshops I was leading and could not find the proper book, I launched into the project of writing what I needed. Now, forty years after those first scribbles in my notebook, I can't seem to find enough time to write all that there is to write! There is always more to say. God continually places before me people who urge me to write something to fill a need.

By using our gifts, we strengthen them. By giving—whether it's a gift of time or talent or money—we continue to receive. Paul was right when he said it doesn't work if we give out of obligation! When we do, we often feel a grudge about giving, and lose the joy.

Giving is actually a form of worship. This is why it is important to give at every opportunity, with an attitude of worship, not just "when the bill comes in." We must give out of love, from the joy of simply giving! God gave us talents to use for God's glory. If we don't use them, they will dry up and be gone in the night. It is through giving that we grow our souls.

Reflect

~ What gift do you have that is lying dormant?

~ What can you do to develop that gift?

~ What gift of time can you use to glorify God? What gift of money?

Pray

Give me the wisdom to know my gifts, O God. You are the source of those gifts, and I thank you for them. I dedicate myself to developing the gifts you have given me for your glory. Amen.

– 50 –

Bloom Where I'm Planted

I have learned to be content whatever the circumstances.
—Philippians 4:11*b* NIV

Some years ago the saying "Bloom where you are planted" was popular. I took that to mean, "Be happy wherever you are." However, I'm learning from my gardening that plants are not always happy where they are. Some plants have need for more sunshine than others, and I've occasionally had the leaves of a plant to scorch in too much sun or to dry out from the wind. And so they must be uprooted and moved. I recently had to dig up a basket full of tulips that were planted too deep. Even given the adversity of the situation and the trauma of transplanting, most of the plants have survived.

It is important for us to make the best of any situation in which we find ourselves. This may mean that we learn to live with a recycled life or with a life that is not as comfortable as it once was.

It has been interesting to observe people as I've moved from place to place during my lifetime. On the street where I live now, we are all new to the community. It was a new subdivision when we bought the house two years ago. Several of our neighbors are retired and moved to the area to be closer to their grown children and grandchildren. Some are couples who bought their first homes and have small children. Some neighbors are single, a young man or woman alone, and some are single parents. We come from several different cultures and races. Each of us has been uprooted and replanted here on our street, most of us willingly but a few not so willingly.

As I walk through our neighborhood, I find some friendly people. Some we've come to know quite well, and we regularly get together for a common meal. Others I've never seen more than once or twice because they never venture out of their houses. My guess is that, if asked, they will tell you that we have an unfriendly neighborhood. I've found in my many neighborhoods that those who are happiest in their present situation are those who take advantage of the circumstances where they find themselves and get to know other people. They don't wait for the world to come to their door, but instead reach out to those around them.

We teach our children these traits, too. I recall a neighbor in one town who had a young daughter, about three years old. I invited them over for coffee one morning, and during our conversation, I learned that the little girl had gone to a birthday party the day before. I inquired about the party, asking her if she had fun. A big grin spread across her face as she began to tell me about what she had done at the party. Then her mother interrupted her and said, "But there was a little girl there who was mean to you. That wasn't much fun!" The three-year-old's smile turned to a frown as she adopted her mother's attitude. The girl had remembered the happy times and ignored the sad one, but now she was being taught in very subtle ways to continually feed on the unhappy situations. She could not bloom if the thorns of unpleasant memories choked her.

I've often wondered what happened to that little girl now that she's in her thirties, hoping that she has not patterned her life after her mother's negative attitude.

I will continue to move plants around, trying to find a better place for them to bloom. But I thank God that they hold on where they are until I find the time to get them in the right places!

Reflect

~ When have you found yourself in a situation that has been hard to live with?

~ What has given you the strength to bloom even under adverse circumstances?

~ How has God recycled a situation for you?

Pray

Thank you, God, for giving me the strength to bloom, no matter what the soil. Help me share those experiences with others and give them encouragement to grow in their own garden plots. Amen.

– 51 –

Too Late

Jesus said, "You may say that there are still four months until harvest time. But I tell you to look, and you will see that the fields are ripe and ready to harvest."

—John 4:35

As I sat on my screened porch, looking out over my garden and the woods beyond, I watched a gentle rain. I thought it would be wise to move some of my indoor plants into the garden to take advantage of the rain, but it was so comfortable on the porch that I put off doing it.

Then I heard a sound in the distance, a sound like prancing horses. It moved closer and closer, when suddenly I realized that the sound was actually prancing raindrops moving through the leaves of the trees. Coming at a steady pace, the sound of the falling raindrops soon reached a thundering cry as the storm emptied itself on the roof over my head.

Too late! It was too late to move the plants into the garden. I would have to water them myself, and they'd not get their leaves washed. God washed the world, but my plants were left out because I procrastinated.

It seems I do this time and time again. I cut some slips from my corkscrew willow and rooted them in water. First the hairlike roots appeared, and then they grew longer and longer. "Those need to go into the ground," I told myself each time I saw them. Soon the leaves on the stems began to wither. Finally, I did put the slips in dirt. Too late! The stems turned black and dried up. If only I had heeded my own words! Now the slips were dead.

I had planned to take a meal to a neighbor who had recently come home from the hospital. I saw her daughter's car drive in and out of the driveway several times a day. "I must fix something and pay her a visit," I reminded myself. Before I knew it, she had recovered enough to be out working in her garden. Too late! I had waited too long to help when it was most needed.

How often we procrastinate and miss a God-given opportunity. We sit there in our pleasure saying, "Maybe later," only to discover that later is too late. The opportunity has passed, and we should have listened to God's nudging. We should have grasped the moment. We should have been alert to what was obviously before our eyes.

Jesus told of the five maidens who said, "I'll fill my lamps later," and went off to greet the wedding party. Another five maidens did not procrastinate, and when the guests of honor arrived, they were prepared. The five who put off the action found that it was too late! Too late to take advantage of the situation. Too late to act as God planned.

Next time I see the gentle rain, I'll try to remember to seize the moment and not wait until it is too late. Will I do the same with the rest of my life?

Reflect

~ When have you missed a golden opportunity to witness to your faith because you put off what you knew God was urging you to do?

~ What opportunity are you likely to postpone that should be seized now? What opportunities in your life could easily be put off?

~ How can you create pride each time you step forward and seize the moment for action?

Pray

Each opportunity you give me is golden, Lord. Help me be alert to those times and make use of them without procrastination. Amen.

– 52 –

Garden Gates

May the Lord make your love increase and overflow for each other and for everyone else, just as ours does for you.

—1 Thessalonians 3:12 NIV

Each time I see a garden gate I am reminded of an experience my daughter had with gates when she was young. When she was in kindergarten she was given a reading readiness test. The test was to register her ability to connect certain word sounds with the letters. Each letter in the alphabet had several pictures beside it, and she was to choose the one that used the letter sound. The proper word for the letter *g* was *gate.* The picture to accompany that word was a small, swinging wooden gate with an arbor of roses over it. You know, the picket-fence–type gate.

Now you have to realize that this child had spent her entire life, except her first two months, living in the ranch country of the western Dakotas. She had absolutely no idea what that picture was about. The only gates in her experience were woven wire gates in the fenced yards of houses or barbed-wire gates that you let down and drove over when visiting friends who lived on ranches.

The designer of that test did not take into account the fact that there are many, many different types of gates, each with its own uniqueness. The teacher also missed an opportunity to introduce the children to the variety of gates.

The Master Designer of the world, however, is very aware of the many designs of people, both physically and spiritually. We must broaden our understanding of each person we meet. As varied as we all are, God wants us to love one another with an overflowing love. If we don't accept and appreciate our differences, we miss the opportunities to grow through our association with these people of God's design. We miss the opportunity to love with an overflowing love.

Reflect

~ How different are your friends, both physically and spiritually?

~ Whom might you search out to get to know better?

~ How can you show God's overflowing love to people who differ from you?

Pray

Thank you, God, for the variety of people you send my way. Help me appreciate their differences and grow as I share your love. Amen.